*Withdrawn from Collection*

# 60-MINUTE
# CEO

# 60-MINUTE CEO

Mastering Leadership an *HOUR* at a Time

## DICK CROSS

bibliomotion
books + media

First published by Bibliomotion, Inc.
39 Harvard Street
Brookline, MA 02445
Tel: 617-934-2427
www.bibliomotion.com

Printed in the United States of America

Library of Congress Cataloging-in-Publication Data

Cross, Dick.
   60-minute CEO : the fast track to top leadership / Dick Cross.
     pages cm
   Summary: "Cross offers executives the fast track to the top leadership position, focusing two aspects: thinking and character. While 60 minutes may seem like a quick fix, three 60-minute sessions a week devoted solely to considering your business and your role as leader are crucial to business and leadership success—and the payoff is proven"— Provided by publisher.
   Includes bibliographical references and index.
   ISBN 978-1-62956-009-0 (hardback) — ISBN 978-1-62956-010-6 (ebook) — ISBN 978-1-62956-011-3 (enhanced ebook)
   1. Leadership.  2. Management.  I. Title.  II. Title: Sixty minute CEO.
HD57.7.C764 2014
658.4'2—dc23
                         2014003387

To loves of my life .... my bride and our daughters,
Jenny, Kate and Hannah

# Contents

## The Captain Has Turned Off the Seatbelt Sign

## Touchdown

# Acknowledgments

In the greatest sense this book is not mine. Rather, it is a collection of ideas either given to me directly, or that others placed me in positions to discover on my own, over three decades.

Together these people are all friends and loved ones.

Sadly deceased, Jack Glover, emeritus Lovett-Learned Professor at Harvard Business School, opened my thinking to an intersection between a young designer's mind and business strategy. Ross Arnold, founder and Managing Partner of Quest Capital, in Atlanta gave me my first and second posts as CEO of underperforming companies. My dear friend Larry Williams, founder and Managing Partner of The Breckenridge Group then followed with a suite of assignments, including my first post at the top of a public company. My best friend from business school, Peter Lamm, then invited me into the newly formed Fenway Partners private equity firm in New York, and entrusted me with a portfolio of seven companies most of which I ran at one time or another. Then Doug Diamond, Managing Partner at Equity South, placed me in the top spot at CARSTAR, Inc. And most recently, Bob Egan and Rodney Eshelman invited me to join Alston Capital Partners and installed me as CEO of that fund's first acquisition.

Along the way, in the fall of 2010, my friend and accountant Tom Gerety introduced me to Jill Friedlander and Erika Heilman, who signed me as what I will always consider their "against-the-odds" first author in what blossomed into a powerhouse portfolio of thought leadership books. With a jaw-dropping stable of authors, who, uncharacteristically and unreservedly, love and know they are overwhelmingly blessed to be under the wings of their publisher.

And most importantly, my bride of four decades and my glorious daughters, Kate and Hannah. Who unselfishly supported a life of maniacal, missionary travel to save businesses, and who held me mercifully to a promise always to be home for weekends.

Thank you for your Love—the greatest gift of all!

# Prepare the Cabin for Takeoff

*Ladies and gentlemen, this is your captain.*

*I am pleased today to welcome you aboard our Transformation Airlines flight from Mediocre Airport in Averageville to Exemplary Field in the City of Exceptional.*

*Today's flight will take us over the peak of Too Tall to Climb Mountain and across the far reaches of the Can't Risk It Valley. As we reach our midpoint, you'll be able to see the Plains of Complacency passing beneath us. After that we'll pick up the Zealous Followership Tailwinds to speed us to our destination.*

*If there is anything that our flight crew can do to make your journey more comfortable, please don't hesitate to ring the overhead bell. It is connected directly to dickcross@crosspartnership.com, where we are waiting at your service.*

*We sincerely hope you enjoy your flight. The weather looks good. And after just a few preflight procedures, we'll be under way.*

# Chapter 1

## *Unmasking the Myth*

These are the facts about how to be great in the Job at the Top. But they're not what most people think.

- Running a business, and doing it extraordinarily well, isn't a full-time job.
- Instead, running a business is an explicit skill that takes dedicated, assiduous thought, and conditioning, and this skill is different from the ones needed for every other job in the company.
- It's easy to learn and fun to do, but it's not taught anywhere except in this book.
- Therefore, many CEOs spend most of their time doing things that have little to do with their highest responsibility, which is running their companies.
- And so they miss the greatest contributions they could possibly make.

On only the rarest of occasions has anyone questioned the following proclamation, which I make at the beginning of most speaking engagements. I believe it without reservation:

*The single greatest determinant of business success is the Job at the Top ... nothing else even comes close!*

Audiences nod thoughtfully, indicating solemn understanding and alignment with what seems to them a near-spiritual truth. What comes next is curious, and perhaps equally predictable. Nonetheless, it's a surprise to everyone else in the room, because it exposes a grand and pervasive charade. And it catches them all in their complicity.

A simple, follow-up question triggers the moment. It's only six words, only one with more than a single syllable.

*How do you run a business?*

No audience has ever offered a response. From the podium I see chins snap up and eyes pop wide in surprise. Then there's an awkward pause. Attention shifts from me as people look at their shoes, befuddled.

I call this *"The Greatest Question Never Asked."* And when I ask individuals rather than audiences, I get the same two reactions. One is incredulity, disbelief that anyone would have the audacity to ask a stranger such a thing. As if I'd asked, "How did life start?" or, "What is love?"

The other reaction is offense. This reaction is typified by the guy whose whole face squinches around the narrow slits his eyes have become. His posture is grim as he sits expressionless behind crossed arms. But then, a light goes off! Reaching clumsily for his wallet, he steps forward. And with relief, he pushes a business card triumphantly into my face: "See, it says it right here…CEO. I know how to do that job!"

The fact is that few of us, even those who've been at it a long time and have generated great results, can explain how we do the Job at the Top.

But I can. Not because I'm any smarter than anyone else, but because it's been my conscious obsession over two and a half decades. I'm passionate about running companies and teaching others how to do it. This obsession has even exceeded my interest in generating exceptional financial results. Fortunately, those results have always followed.

The next chapter takes a hard look at the customs we take for granted as "truths" about how to do the Job at the Top. These are things we seldom even consider questioning. But they're also things that we know aren't getting the job done. The chapter addresses directly, not obliquely, challenges we seldom discuss, except in confidence with others who are facing situations like our own: how to motivate our teams to higher achievement; how to move our businesses forward at the pace and with the performance we've committed to. Chapter 2 opens you up to questioning the ideals and the models we've elevated to the status of "natural law" in running our organizations.

Chapter 3 lays out a simple, fresh, and effective framework for how to approach the Job at the Top. It's a zoomed-out version of a road map for getting good—really good—at it in less time than you'd ever imagined. Subsequent chapters zoom back in to give you focused views of more specific headings, food along the trail, and waypoints for your journey.

With chapters 2 and 3 laying the foundation, chapter 4 delivers the punch: how to do the Job at the Top better, more easily, and more joyfully than most of us ever have imagined it could be done.

The best way to read this book is to take your time and fully digest the next three chapters. Read them carefully, because they set up everything that follows. You may even want to read them more than once. Stop from time to time to ask yourself, "Is this really sinking in and making sense to me?" Absorb the material until you have no trouble recalling the simple principles laid out and seeing the key points in your head.

Then you can just browse through the rest of the book and pick any chapter that captures your imagination. Perhaps a specific chapter addresses a situation you're currently facing. Or you might feel compelled to read straight through. However you decide to approach the *60-Minute CEO*, spending time with this book will deepen your thoughtfulness and your understanding of how to perform exceptionally well in the Job at the Top. It will coach you on how to refine your skills. And it will show you how to talk about the method and how to teach it to other people in your company, in your church group, or maybe even in your family.

My greatest hope is not to wow you with some great new theory. Rather, it's to bring into your consciousness things you probably already know deep down inside. Those things make sense to you the instant you read about them. But you seldom think about them in any disciplined way, nor do you spend time building them explicitly into the way you approach your job.

It's easier than you think. It works. And it's fun. Good luck!

# Chapter 2

## *Softening Up the Beachhead*

Here's the setup for what's to come and why I believe it. The fact is that I have yet to find a business school curriculum that includes a course titled: "How to Run a Business." Sure, there are plenty of courses on how to do every other job in the company: marketing, sales, human resources, plant management, procurement, and the rest. But there's not a course for the Job at the Top.

Why not?

Because the Job at the Top is the omnibus responsibility. It's the umbrella that covers everything a company does. Asking for an answer to an all-encompassing question like "How do you run a company?" covers so much ground that our reflex response shifts us into a Newtonian "parts-to-whole" rather than a "whole-to-parts" way of looking at the world (more on this later). This channels us into the way Western culture approaches just about anything that's complex...we disaggregate a complex thing into its subparts with the idea that if we can understand the parts, we will understand the whole and how it works.

It follows, then, that two years in business school spent scrutinizing the subcomponents of businesses will come together one fine day in June, resulting in the graduate knowing how to run a company! If you're one of those unfortunates who has gotten a job running a company just after that glorious June day, you know one thing. That's a lousy idea!

Regrettably, our only other route to mastery in the Job at the Top is to spend years, maybe decades, working for others—who probably aren't very good at their jobs—and figure it out that way! I say, good luck!

This book offers an alternative. It addresses the whole of the question, "How do I master the Job at the Top?" with a prescription that, at first glance, seems like heresy because it runs counter to the Newtonian way of thinking. But also because it creates a big stain on a considerable backdrop of precedent and upon the model on which we've imprinted, one our fathers and grandfathers brought home with them from their experiences in the Second World War.

Jack Glover, managing partner of the Cambridge Institute (my first management consulting firm), the Lovett-Learned Chair at Harvard Business School, and my favorite mentor, described it this way:

> *The strongest influence on a manager's style is the style of*
> *the first manager he served.*

So strong is our need, at that early, uncertain stage of our career, for a model of someone we deem successful that we tend to imprint, as Jack would say, on our first boss. And in the early 1940s nearly every able-bodied person aged eighteen to twenty-four experienced his first model of organizational authority in the military. And with that model, they won a war!

It should come as no surprise, then, that a whole generation of young men and women, returning from victory and ready to launch their own careers and lives, ran their businesses and their families according to the principles of command and control. Nor is it surprising that their kids would imprint on those methods. Then their kids, and so on.

But the model you're about to read breaks the string. It flies in the face of nearly everything we've learned about how to do the Job at the Top from our predecessors. But it works. And it works better than the old model, these days. And it comes just in time.

Just in time? Yes. Because today we are four generations away from the precedent set in World War II. That's enough time for the original imprinting to fade. And enough time for new societal mores to arise, including unprecedented expectations for individual self-worth versus material worth and individual choice versus blind subservience.

With these events, the command-and-control model has outlived its time. Obsolete along with it, most notably, is the central idea that the person at the top is supposed to "control" the organization by simple virtue of the authority vested in the position. A corollary is that control comes through the premise that the person at the top knows more than anyone else about the business.

Among the underpinnings of the new model, the one that works today, are these:

- The Job at the Top is no longer to control, but rather to enable.
- The Job at the Top is no longer to make decisions, but rather to foster great decision making in all the other parts of the organization.
- The Job at the Top is no longer to demand performance, but rather to instill zealous drive for performance in everyone else.
- The Job at the Top is no longer to enforce constructive behavior, but rather to inspire it.

Ever find yourself asking, "What's wrong with younger people these days? Particularly the gen Xers, gen Yers, and, oh yeah, the millennials? Why aren't they more like we were at that stage of our careers? We were glad to have a job and willing to do just about anything to keep it and advance?"

The next two chapters offer a framework for answering those questions.

# Chapter 3

## *The Big Idea*

It would be too great a stretch to present what you're about to read as science. Because the data was collected serially and in an undisciplined way over a twenty-year period, it can hardly be considered a controlled experiment. Also, you can't verify the product with statistics. But for me, all the data points line up, and together they explain a lot about what works and what doesn't work throughout the course of a career. Now I want to share that understanding with you.

Through my speaking and consulting, I've learned that there are lots of others—maybe even you—who are in the same boat I was, lacking confidence in the job they're doing. And they really aren't in a position to evaluate their pluses and minuses against any standards other than purely financial ones. No other standards exist for the Job at the Top. This leaves us to proceed hoping that we are doing a great job. But it also leaves us carrying deep concerns that we might be doing better. That's an admission we can't discuss with anyone. Not our reports. Not our investors or bankers. Usually not even with our families and friends.

So, my intention is to help you see over the gunnels. I'll offer you relevant and reliable reference points for how to do your Job at the Top—and how to do it well. These points may help you advance your methods, and will certainly give you a greater degree of comfort at the helm. But you are not the only one who will feel the good effects. Your increased comfort level will cause others to feel greater confidence in your leadership, as well as greater satisfaction that they are part of your organization.

One of the jaw-droppers I deliver in my speeches—and one with which everyone agrees once it's out—is how simple it is to do a great Job at the Top. It's one of those things that everyone feels he should have known, but just never saw in such clear light before.

The logic for that conclusion falls under two main headings: these are *thinking* and *character*.

*Thinking/Character Diagram*

## Thinking

Half of the Job at the Top is about *thinking*. When I say that to audiences, what I see on most of the faces in the footlights is puzzlement, broken up by relief on some faces. And it's the second group I worry about most.

Those are the people who believe that thinking is easy. That it's not real work. Maybe because it doesn't make you sweat or swear or because it doesn't produce immediately measurable results. Or perhaps because it doesn't appear to others like it's contributing anything while it's going on, so they ignore it and spend their time doing "things that matter" more. Mostly, as it turns out, they spend their time doing things they were good at before they got their Jobs at the Top. Now, really, those things ought to be done by others.

It's a phenomenon we all know. Ex-accountant CEOs huddle in their offices with spreadsheets. Ex-salespeople jam their calendars with customer calls. Old operators haunt the plant floors and sit in on production meetings. R&D types fiddle with the next innovation. You get the idea.

Why is it so tempting to revert to your well-worn path? Because thinking broadly about your business...*thinking like a CEO*...is hard work, particularly when there is no reliable framework to guide the process, as there is for nearly every other activity in a company.

But the quality of thinking in the Job at the Top—about how productively all the parts of the business fit together and about how the whole business fits into the world around it—is the anchor point for sustainable vibrancy. And the person in the Job at the Top is the only one in the company paid to do that kind of thinking.

In companies where this kind of thinking doesn't occur, rates of survival and levels of ultimate success are lower. Affiliations with these businesses become increasingly dissatisfying for workers, customers, and others upon whom they depend. Those relationships eventually end.

But this need not be the case. In the next chapter I'll give you a proven and overarching set of guidelines for how to think like a CEO, which will make the process easier and even fun. As you read on, you'll begin collecting a portfolio of more specific perspectives and techniques for thinking like a CEO, and for doing it well, which you can put to use immediately.

If you embrace these ideas and build them into your consciousness, you'll be well on your way toward doing your Job at the Top better than 90 percent of the people running businesses today.

That will carry us to the halfway mark of this book. Once we're there, we'll tackle the second part of the prescription for doing a great Job at the Top, which focuses on *character*.

## Character

The second half of the formula for greatness in your Job at the Top involves character. Your personal character. You might ask, "What about my character? I'm in charge. Who's going to challenge my character?" Or, more regrettably, "I pay everyone else. Doesn't that mean they just have to put up with me?"

Unfortunately, far too many people in Jobs at the Top believe that's the case. But they're wrong. Personal character at the top determines the commitment of the organization's followership. The character of those at the top is scrutinized at a level entirely underestimated by most CEOs. As CEO, your expressions, words, emotions, and activities are constantly evaluated, by your people, your customers, and others in your work community. The conclusions, confirmed by countless around-the-watercooler chats about you, constitute employees' baseline for how much to trust you. And similar evaluations determine how much your customers, vendors, and others in your network trust your business. Then, following their evaluations, these people decide how much of themselves to give to you. Do they choose to invest the minimum required to maintain the relationship? Do they stay with you until a better option comes along? Or do they commit their entire heart and soul to supporting you in achieving your intentions? It's your choice, and it depends largely upon your personal character.

Loyalty in organizations is principally about character at the top. Great thinking without continuous attention to aspirational character at the top—the kind that cultivates a zealous following—leaves a lot on the table.

Just think for a moment about people like George Washington, Abraham Lincoln, Sir Ernest Shackleton, Winston Churchill, Douglas MacArthur, Martin Luther King Jr., Billy Graham, and Benazir Bhutto. These people's lives weren't about metrics of performance or personal wealth. Their lives were about character, character that inspired countless others to be better than they would have been otherwise. These heroes inspired those who followed with the principles of character they talked about, demonstrated, and reinforced through their every thought and action.

You probably have felt the influence of a person like this at the helm, in a company where the atmosphere is electric. At such companies, everyone seems energetically locked together to accomplish something great. Compare these companies with the businesses that feel dull, and seem to be filled with uninspired people simply enduring a day at work in order to go away and do something else.

Which type is your company?

What is the difference between these two extremes? I hope you already see what's coming, and that you are sitting down, because … *it's you!*

People who are best at demonstrating the kind of character that inspires others to be better than they would be otherwise come across as authentic, easy to understand, and predictable. They are anchored to principles that everyone admires, and which they protect regardless of the circumstances.

And how do top CEOs convey these attributes? At one end of the spectrum it's through the tiniest details in their everyday behavior. And at the other, it's in how they handle the gravest moments of truth.

People are watching you navigate both ends, and every point in between, more carefully than you'd ever imagine. They are looking for signals of your character, and they're assessing the degree to which your vision and what you care about most match their own aspirations. When the signals are clear and consistent and the match is good, the atmosphere is charged with an optimism and electricity not found anywhere else.

It sounds difficult: you must pay constant, scrupulous attention to the way you are being perceived. But it's not hard. In fact, it's one of the most fascinating and joyous gifts of your position. Living out your commitment to character does take your conscious attention, however, as well as the humility to evaluate yourself continually in the harshest of lights. In later chapters we'll talk more about how to do those exact things.

# Chapter 4

## *60 Minutes... Really?*

The biggest gasps I provoke, along with the coldest looks, come when I offer my opinion that the Job at the Top is less than a full-time occupation. Dramatically less.

In chapter 3, under the heading "Thinking," I made the point that most CEOs spend considerable time doing things they knew how to do before they got their current jobs: financial management, sales, production, R&D, and the like. A significant portion of the rest of their time is taken up informing outsiders—including investors, lenders, trade press, suppliers, and the government—about the state of the company, a task that often spurs debilitating stress because of a need to paint a picture that's better than reality. The remainder of a CEO's time is typically devoted to administrative responsibilities, such as approving documents, updating the team, approving others' decisions, and serving as the official spokesperson for the organization.

Maybe I'm leaving something out, but generally, heads in big audiences are bobbing about now. Invariably, some members of the audience are rolling their eyes about what a "load" it all is.

Sit down again, because here comes another showstopper.

None of those responsibilities has much at all to do with your Job at the Top, in running the company. They don't have much at all to do with what you are getting paid to do, which is to drive the future trajectory of the business. You must drive the business to new heights. You must foresee and navigate pitfalls. And you must ensure that the successes you achieve continue over a long period of time.

Achieving those outcomes is your highest calling in the Job at the Top. It's not about the other stuff, which, in all but the smallest organizations, could and should be assigned to someone else.

Assuring these outcomes over a sustained period of time is a heavy burden indeed, but there's also great news.

Big-picture thinking and the conscious attention to character that fuel the momentum of the business—the highest calling of your Job at the Top—don't constitute a full-time occupation. In fact, these things are done most effectively in small but frequent and concentrated sessions, leaving plenty of space for whatever you choose to do with the rest of your time.

But this deep thinking and living with character are requisites for responsible performance at the top. They take time and your assiduous concentration. And there is a learning curve.

Thinking like a CEO is like starting a swimming regimen. At the outset, you can't complete a lot of laps. Your stroke feels choppy, anything but fluid, and for a while you wonder if you're getting anywhere. But, with persistence, your endurance, your commitment, and your joy build. Your stroke improves and becomes more natural. You start having brief moments when you feel the water rushing in your wake, effortlessly. Eventually, you reach a point where your swim time and the high it gives you are things that you have built into your life and that you depend upon for a healthy outlook, continued effectiveness, and personal growth. Not many swimmers train for more than an hour at a time. Nor do they need to, if their efforts are consistent and intensely concentrated.

Being a great CEO is just like that.

If you start with twenty minutes, three days a week, of focused concentration on the big picture of your business and on the character you transmit, you'll eventually build up to an hour. Along the way, you'll find yourself more energized and you'll know that you're doing better in your job. Once you reach your plateau, you'll begin seeing things you've never seen before. You'll put previously independent insights together to create new depths of understanding about what makes your company tick, and about how to make it tick faster and louder. You'll move through unforeseen crises more easily and with less stress. You'll feel a new confidence in yourself. You'll feel the authentic support of your organization in ways you haven't felt before. And you'll love it.

On the outside chance that spending sixty minutes three days a week thinking quietly just isn't your thing...well, my view is a harsh one. If that is the case, your only responsible action—for your company, its ownership, your employees, and everyone else the business touches—is to step down and let someone else do the job.

It's that important.

But it's too early for you to even think about that kind of outcome. Instead, read on about how, specifically, to:

- Think effectively about the whole of your business and its future trajectory
- Handle yourself in ways that build a devoted following of people who are joyfully giving you their all

So start now.

Block out three twenty-minute sessions per week. Use the readings that follow as grist for your thinking during those sessions. Then expand them. Before long, certain practices and traits you're reading about will begin to appear in your behavior. People in your organization will notice them and become more committed to you. They'll become more effective in their jobs, and you'll be doing a better Job at the Top.

# Climbing Through 10,000 Feet

*Ladies and gentlemen, this is your lead flight attendant. After a smooth takeoff, we are climbing through ten thousand feet on our way to a cruise altitude of thirty-nine thousand feet. At this time it is permissible to use your electronic devices. In just a few minutes the crew will begin passing down the aisles with complimentary snacks and beverages. But please stay seated until the captain switches off the seatbelt sign.*

*Our remaining flight time will be a brief sixty minutes. So please relax, and use this time without distractions to think deeply about the first half of your Job at the Top . . . how to think like a CEO.*

# Chapter 5

## *Thinking... About What?*

Chapter 3 made the argument that half of the Job at the Top is about thinking... thinking about the whole of your business.

But thinking about the whole of a business, rather than in the part-at-a-time Newtonian way, is such a broad assignment that most people have a hard time even getting started. Over twenty-five years my firm, The Cross Partnership, has observed that most CEOs spend 95 to 100 percent of their time doing things other than disciplined thinking about the whole of their businesses. Yet, that's what it takes to do the job: time spent alone, undistracted by phones, e-mail, or conversation, for periods of a half hour or more, thinking about the degree to which the business is realizing its full potential.

But that shouldn't be a surprise. Because we humans have a tendency to get distracted. Without reliable frameworks to guide our thinking about complicated things, we generally don't do it. Rather, we find easier things to occupy our time. At the same time, we acknowledge that the things we can't make ourselves think about just might be the most important aspects of our lives!

So, what follows is a framework for thinking about the whole of your business that makes it easy and even fun. It's a list of only two questions that build upon one another. And the more frequently you revisit them, the richer your fascination will grow with the big picture of your enterprise.

For many, the sixty-minute habit becomes a narcotic. It's a time when things come to you magically. A time when you see things about your business that you and everyone else around you are missing in the course of your usual workdays. These are things that could separate you from the pack, things that could make your business truly great! Honing in on these differentiators is one of the reasons we CEOs get paid more than anyone else for what we do. And this is an easy way to fulfill that responsibility.

Start with just twenty minutes alone—and build up to an hour—and you will find your sessions becoming the most regenerative, refreshing moments of your week. The clarity of your big-picture thinking will become the backdrop for everything else you do at work. Involuntarily, it will creep into both the most obvious and most subtle ways you handle yourself. And in less time than you might imagine, you'll start seeing others align their behavior more perfectly with what you believe is best for your business.

When you start out, spending time with each of the two key questions will be an exercise in itself. But before long you will begin to see the bridges that link these separate inquiries. And in many instances, these links are where you will discover compelling insights that give you a new, multidimensional grip on making your business all that it can be.

### Question 1: *"What is my business today, and does it still make as much sense as it used to?"*

Most of us run businesses that have been around for a while. Some run companies that launched just a year or so ago. Regardless of the business's history, this same "What is my business?" thinking exercise applies. Why? Because the mismatch between (1) the inherent "stickiness" of things we set in place in our organizations and (2) the accelerating pace of change in the world around us keeps us continually out of date. A strategy, goal, or product that might have made perfect sense just six months ago may already be hopelessly ineffective. And what was put in place five years ago almost certainly is!

So, this first angle on thinking in your Job at the Top is to continually question the relevance of what's going on in your business from two perspectives. First, does what's going on *inside* make as much sense as it used to? For example, if we've made changes in one part of the system, are all the other pieces still performing optimally and fitting together with minimal friction, generating maximum productivity? And second, does everything that's occurring on the inside still have as much punch as it once did on the *outside?* That is, does it still impress your customers and your influencers, and outperform your competition?

Here are some tips to get your thinking headed in the right direction on both these fronts:

Does what's going on *inside* make as much sense as it used to?

- Where are the points of friction in my organization?
- In what aspects are we less effective today than before? How are we more effective?
- What parts of my organization are holding others back?
- Where is morale lower—or higher—than before, and why?
- Where are we losing business, productivity, and profitability, and why? Where are we gaining?
- What's our untapped potential, and what would it take to unlock it?

Does my business still have as much "punch" on the *outside* as it used to?

- What are my sales and gross margin trajectories, and why?
- Am I experiencing greater price pressure?

- What are my share positions now versus before, with different customer segments?
- Which products and services are growing and which are not? Why?
- Am I still getting as much positive press as I used to get?
- Am I attracting a growing number of new customers?
- Are people asking my advice?
- Are people talking about my business?
- Am I number one in my market for what I do?
- Am I as confident and proud when I'm talking about my business as I used to be?
- Why do people continue to do business with me…is it any different from before? Have any customers stopped? Why?

No one else in the organization has the responsibility for consolidating this kind of thinking into an overarching picture of the current health of your business. It's all yours. Failing to do it is a choice to abdicate the future of your business to the wiles of others.

### Question 2: *"Where is my business today, and where does it need to be?"*

I define business positioning as the intersection of three factors: customers, competitors, and technology. Regrettably, we don't control any of them. Each moves independently. And today, each moves more rapidly, less homogeneously, and less predictably than ever before.

Failure to continuously adjust the positioning of your business so that you are synchronized with all this movement leads inevitably to obsolescence and irrelevance. For some businesses it's a very short journey. For others, it might take decades. The pace is set by the speed with which customers' preferences, competitors' offerings, and relevant technologies are changing. Unless you are paying continuous attention to moving your business from where it's been to where it needs to be with regard to changes in these externalities, your business will decline. Eventually, it will disappear.

Here as well, no one else in your organization is vested with the responsibility for this kind of thinking. It's all yours.

In the early 1970s Bruce Henderson, then a professor at the Harvard Business School, posed a theory about the phenomenon of sustainability in business, which we'll discuss in greater detail in chapter 13. He observed that the lives of businesses are like those of biological organisms. Businesses, too, follow a natural four-stage life cycle, going from embryonic start-ups through a growth stage, then to maturity and eventually to aging and decline. And there are lots of casualties along the way, businesses that failed to progress from one stage to the next. But unlike biological organisms, the life cycle in businesses can be managed to adjust the pace of the mutations, to improve the odds of survival through the journey, and, in fact, to interrupt and even reverse the otherwise natural progression toward the inevitable endings of people and animals.

The single greatest determinant of which path your business follows—either the normal biological progression toward entropy or the route on which your business gains strength and vibrance with each new stage and extends the time frame of its relevance, perhaps indefinitely? It's **you!**

# Chapter 6

## *Chameleon at the Top*

Why do so many CEOs fail to drive their businesses successfully through the stages of the life cycle, extending both
their time and the rewards along the way? Why are there so many
stories of businesses disappointingly stuck and of so many casualties...ill-fated alpinists...on the slopes of their curves?

It's because the orientation in the Job at the Top needs to shift
as a business moves through the phases of the life cycle. What
works best in the embryonic phase doesn't work in the growth
zone. Growth business practices fail in maturity and aging.

Here's how that works.

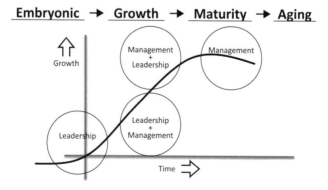

• In the embryonic stage, the leading characteristic a CEO needs in order to launch an enterprise is charismatic leadership. It's that magnetic quality that attracts others to join a quest that's exciting, but also one that everyone knows debarks into risky, uncharted territory. This charismatic leadership style is integrative, projective, optimistic, and dauntless. A CEO with this style fearlessly ignores signals that may cause others to cower. She fills her mind, and the minds of those around her, with what could be, not concerning herself with what might not. Timidity is the enemy of innovation.

• When an emergent business takes hold and begins to transition from the embryonic into the growth stage, the orientation in the Job at the Top needs to shift as well. In the early part of the growth phase, this means adding a dose of managerial perspective to balance the charismatic leadership and to deal with the pragmatic realities and the increasing administrative and strategic complexity of an emerging enterprise. Finding and adding this kind of talent is the easy part. The tougher hurdle—a lot tougher for most early-stage CEOs—is truly accepting it. Far too often, the new resource is positioned as an isolated appurtenance rather than as a necessary partner in running the business. It takes humility on the part of the charismatic leader, a tall order for many, to embrace the new executive's perspective as a critical complement to that of the freer-wheeling, bigger-than-life character who started the business. As the business then molts from early growth into a larger growth enterprise, the shift from charismatic leadership toward management at the top needs to take another step forward. Here, the early-stage growth CEO must anticipate and encourage more pragmatic and analytical perspectives in more and more situations.

• Some CEOs transform themselves and carry their effectiveness gracefully from the embryonic stage through the growth stage and beyond. But the statistics on new business failures indicate that this is not the norm. The 40 to 50 percent three-year

failure rate among American startups—together with the unmea-
sured percentage of our six million American businesses stuck at
levels of achievement well below their potentials—suggests that
bridging the gap between the embryonic and growth stages is not
to be taken for granted. It deserves the CEOs explicit attention: to
be both acutely aware of the progression of his business as it molts
from the embryonic through the growth stages, and to adjust and
match his approach to his Job at the Top with what works. Continually adjusting the charismatic-pragmatic cocktail at the top.
Exhibiting the humility that encourages others to take the lead
where their judgment exceeds.

- In a company's mature stage, and beyond, the shift
toward the pragmatic, disciplined and managerial perspective
becomes almost complete. Success in mature businesses turns
on the relentless refinement of processes and on continuous, if
only slight, improvements of precision in products and operations
rather than on new, broad, creative strokes. The top leadership
role in the mature stage is more about steadily maintaining the
brand, the image, the core values, the purpose, and the morale of
the business, rather than heroic reimagining of the fundamental
concept and gaining committed followership.

Take this message to heart and be constantly aware of the life
cycle stage of your business. Ideally, you will adjust your style to
drive your organization across the gaps. Make it a priority to think
explicitly about matching your approach to your Job at the Top
with the positioning of your business in your sixty minutes three
times a week. At what stage is your business? What do you need to
be in order to captain your business effectively through the straits
of transformation? If you do this critical thinking, you'll have a
solid chance of being one of the few who makes the transitions
successfully.

# Chapter 7

## *Your Big Picture on the Back of an Envelope*

Earlier, I made the point that half the Job at the Top is about thinking. And I hinted that it is seldom done well, or at least it's not done as well as it should be, because thinking about the business in a big-picture way seems hard. Since there are other things to distract our attention, we tend to focus on the easier tasks that are seen by others as contributing more.

The truth? Thinking, as a general practice, isn't hard. It's joyous. It just becomes hard when we have no guidelines or framework to follow, no familiar paths we trust. In contrast, mental wandering isn't fulfilling. It feels like a waste of time. When we don't have thought models to follow, we don't think fruitfully.

Imagine for a moment that there are no frameworks for a P&L, a balance sheet, or a cash flow report, yet you have a nagging concern about the financial health of your business. You'd get the same unproductive result that you get when your thinking has no guide. There would be no reliable frameworks for thinking about the business's finances. No path to follow. So you'd probably put it off. The reason we spend so much time with spreadsheets and the other "forms" that are part of running a business? It's simply because they're there! Thinking is fun when we have a reliable framework to guide us.

Until now, there's been no equivalent to the frameworks we have for thinking about other parts of our businesses; there's been no framework that makes it easy, and even fun, for us to think, explicitly, about *the greatest determinant of business success...the Job at the Top!*

In this chapter I'll introduce you to one framework for thinking explicitly about your Job at the Top (in addition to the two key questions posed in chapter 5), and we'll look at how it fits in as the linchpin and the accelerant for everything else in your company. I call this framework the Back of the Envelope. I wrote about this in my book *Just Run It!*, a template for creating an exceptional business. If you read about the Back of the Envelope there, consider this a refresher for your sixty-minute sessions. It's important enough to repeat.

The idea came to me late on a Friday night flight after a week of visiting six acquisition prospects for a group of very smart Boston investors. My briefcase was bursting with business plans, industry studies, historical financials, and interview notes. And I was scared. I didn't know how I was going to make sense of everything I'd collected before I met Monday morning with my clients, who I now was convinced had agreed to pay me way too much for what I was going to tell them.

Under the dim, yellow glow of the overhead lights I began to sketch. I'd gone to undergraduate and graduate school for architecture before attending business school, so sketching helps me think. A drawing emerged on my yellow pad, though I didn't know exactly why at first.

It was the back of a standard number 10 envelope. As the composition of four triangles flowed out of my pencil, my attention exploded into another realm, crashing through a dark curtain into a bright room of unimaginable scale and wonder.

In the left-hand triangle I quickly wrote *Customers*. I wasn't thinking about demographics the way everyone defines them, but rather about what each company's customers really cared about most.

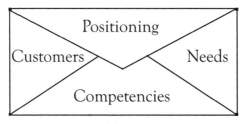

*Back of the Envelope*

To the right I wrote *Needs*. Which of those customers' most important needs might each company be able to address? Maybe some of these were things that seemed far afield from what the company actually sold.

Racing to the top, I wrote *Positioning*. How would each company have to be viewed by its customers in order to be the inarguable first choice to help them with something they cared about?

And in the bottom triangle I wrote *Competencies*. What capabilities and resources would each business need in order to deliver convincingly and consistently on the story I'd created for it? And were those competencies within the realm of reason?

Predictably, all of my first ideas were "no goes." The initial parts of the stories for each candidate—the parts on Customers, Needs, and Positioning—were attractive prospects. But in each case my initial stories crashed full throttle into a concrete retaining wall of reality when I got to the triangle labeled Competencies. At first glance, every initial possibility seemed clearly out of reasonable reach for each business.

But I was fully caffeinated, having fun, and on a roll. With each subsequent pass around the envelope I saw new stories unfold for each business. By the time the wheels hit the tarmac at Boston Logan, I knew which businesses had compelling prospects, what would be required to achieve those prospects, and how significant the results might be.

All from a sketch on the Back of an Envelope.

Try this for yourself. During your initial sixty-minute think-ing sessions, concentrate on this exercise. Draw the Envelope and fill in the triangles for your business, examining your "Custom-ers" (what they care about), "Needs" (what you can do for them), "Positioning" (how you have to be viewed in order to be your cus-tomers' first choice), and "Competencies" (what it takes for your company to fulfill your customers' expectations). Expect to make lots of passes and to throw lots of balled-up sheets into the trash. Don't worry. That's the way it's supposed to work. But if you per-sist, the odds are high that you'll begin seeing things about your business that you hadn't seen before.

You'll be thinking like a CEO.

# Chapter 8

## *What Your Customers Want...*
## *Right Now!*

If you've read chapter 7, "Your Big Picture on the Back of an Envelope," you'll recall that I described the right way to think about customers, not according to who they are—their demographics—but rather according to what's important to them.

You need to look far beyond the boundaries of what you sell them for clues to what they really care about.

Here's the logic.

Twenty years ago, we could segment people into groups and pretty much understand what it would take to win their business by looking at correlations between their past buying behaviors and things like age, income, geographical region, family, purchasing history, ethnicity, and so on. Decision modeling—correlating observations from the past to predict future behaviors—had come on the scene in the mid-1960s and had taken business analytics by storm. Complemented by the concurrent emergence of low-cost computational power, decision modeling became the standard approach to projecting people's proclivities for buying things and, by extension, for how to sell to them.

But the Internet is now making obsolete most of the inferential and sample-based logic we've used to predict consumer-buying behaviors for more than half a century. Customers now enjoy immediate access to all the information they want about virtually everything they want to buy. They can consult electronic communities of reviewers that are much more credible than marketers, and which reach far beyond the older and narrower circles of influence created through advertising. And they can do all this without leaving home!

The result is that the buying behavior of consumers, who are now armed with more detailed and credible information, is not as easily categorized into homogeneous and predictable groups. Those who may seem identical in demographic respects may be as different from one another as a skinhead and a priest in terms of what they care about, and what they want to buy and why.

So now how do we identify cohesive markets? How do we reach people who will respond similarly to the same stimuli from businesses like ours? How can we get them to want our goods?

We need to look more directly through the lenses of "indicators" into how people think, by focusing on them as emotionally unique decision makers rather than as a member of a larger group of outwardly similar beings. We need to look at them as lives that we may be able to improve rather than as "transactions." How? By talking to them. By reading about them. And by looking beyond the hits on our websites into what might be driving them to our businesses in the first place. These are the "indicators" that we must focus on, rather than the location or age of the customer. We must commit to adjusting our businesses to match our continually growing understanding of what customers care about most. What worked in the past, and our allegiance to it, really shouldn't give us much confidence that we'll continue to be our customers' unquestionable first choice anymore. Understanding what people care about is now our most solid beachhead for building loyal customer relationships that also result in those people promoting us to their friends and others who think like they think.

So here are some implications.

First, I'd be quite surprised if your current customers don't represent a wide range of patterns regarding what they care about most. That's no problem; the diversity of your customer base and what they care about today are simply reflections of those interests you have captured, likely largely unintentionally, in the past.

Consider for a moment what your customer base might look like if you committed to addressing the most important cares of a large pool of homogeneous thinkers more accurately and compellingly. My bet is that you'd have more customers. From the outside, they might look very different from one another, but if you appeal to what they care about most on the inside, they'll be more loyal. And you probably wouldn't lose any of the legacy outliers—until the time when someone else who addresses their cares more explicitly comes along.

In your focused sixty-minute sessions, start thinking a few layers below the demographics of your customers. Consider what they care about most. The time you spend talking directly to your customers, asking why they are your supporters and what they really care about, can be your brightest guide lights for continued relevance. Become a student of contemporary thought and culture, because they're changing across all age groups. Unless you seize the helm and change your course to go with this cultural change, your customers will go elsewhere.

Once you see the patterns, let your target audience know that you care about the same things they do. Maybe their needs are only tangentially related to what you sell them. Maybe they're not related at all. It doesn't matter. Your job is about matching their experiences with your business to the things they care about most. Today's customers care about customer service so provide fresh, super-premium coffee they might pay $3 for elsewhere (nothing says "I don't care about you" louder than stale coffee). Consider all aspects of their experience, like how they are greeted at your door and how your goods are packaged. Even send them thank-you notes. Host informal gatherings that create a community of followers. This style of thinking is the linchpin for unimaginable results, and it is your responsibility.

## Ideas for Conveying That You Care

- Congratulate customers—for a new baby, wedding, college graduation, honor roll, civic appointment, having run a marathon, etc.—on your website, and let them know.
- Give tickets to the theater or a ball game...no contests, just offer an occasional gift.
- Offer to sponsor customers to join a group you support that's also of interest to them.
- Hang a bulletin board in your lobby for customer photos.
- Sponsor local ads thanking and naming customers.
- Offer to support favorite community events of your customers.
- Give wedding and baby gifts.
- Underwrite a speaker series with cocktails for customers in your place of business.
- Create periodic special offers for selected customers grouped by common interests.
- Establish a customer advisory board.
- Ask customers with specific expertise—lawyers, real estate agents, business consultants, bankers—for informal advice.
- Offer your premises for customer events.

# Chapter 9

## *It's Not Your Products Anymore*

I find many businesses that are coaxing customers through their doors with attributes that have very little to do with what those businesses think they're selling. These are customers who come for what I call "collateral benefits."

Because features, functions, quality, convenience, and price are still so ingrained in our thinking as the dominant factors in selling, we fail to even consider all the other things that might be influencing customers' decisions about who to reward with their business. Again, largely because of the Internet—which links us to immediate substitutes with comparable features, functions, quality, convenience, and price for nearly everything we want—other factors are rising rapidly as the pivot points for purchasing decisions.

So what do you do?

Start by making a list of what you believe your target customers care about most. Include things that are beyond—way beyond—the boundaries of what you sell them. For some businesses this might mean connecting with customers through interest in their kids, their favorite places, or their hobbies. Salespeople should ask questions about customers' personal lives and take notes to remember recent conversations, so they can continue the dialogue in the next encounter. Nordstrom raised this sales technique to a high art. Other businesses might find that their customers care about golf or cars or politics or a certain charity. Encourage your employees to record and remember those things, and ask them to talk with your customers about these interests at every opportunity. The technique of "wrapping" what you sell with an organization-wide personal interest in the lives of customers works every time.

For example, nearly everyone needs a local service station. And nearly everyone has multiple options for where to buy gas and have minor maintenance and repairs done, and these options typically have comparable pricing, service, quality, and convenience. So what makes us choose one station over another? It's something different from the fuel, oil changes, and wipers we actually pay for. There's something in addition. And usually that something touches us in a place we need to be touched; it might be a friendly smile, an attendant who knows your name, or a mechanic who gives free maintenance tips or who chats about a hobby, family, or local news.

Next, begin imagining and listing all the ways you might adjust the experience your business delivers to match up with your customers' greatest interests.

This means rethinking how you make customers feel every time you "touch" them: on phone calls; with the look and navigation of your website; through the design and atmosphere of your premises; with the way customers or other visitors are greeted; and through the things you can give them "for free" that they'll appreciate. Sometimes the positive differentiator is no more than knowing customers' names and smiling at them. Your willingness to do whatever it takes to make something right for them, or someone they care about, must shine through. Don't underestimate the impact that your positive contributions in the communities you serve can have on your customers' feelings about your business. Your support of these nonbusiness causes can bring customers to your door as well.

Shift your focus from *transactions* to the total *persona* of your business. Think about how well this persona endears you to the people you care about most—by matching up with what they care about most. Because today—unless you control a truly unique offering that a lot of people need—the persona of your business is the only matchless advantage you've got.

## The Personas of Thriving Businesses

- Ben & Jerry's—on the vanguard of doing good
- Southwest Airlines—lightheartedness that delivers
- Ritz-Carlton—ladies and gentlemen serving ladies and gentlemen
- Apple—the ultimate in cool and friendly
- Rolex—old-school class
- Facebook—personal connection
- Levi's—there's a cowboy in all of us
- Zappos—friendly shoe salesperson with a warehouse of choice in your own home

We all talk a lot about brand these days. But most of our "brand talk" misses the point. Brand is not about your logo or your tagline or your theme song. Nor is it usually about the attributes of what, specifically, you sell. Brand these days is about the emotional reaction your company triggers in the minds of the individuals you care about most, your customers.

Mike Toth, a dear friend and icon of branding in the toughest industry of all—fashion, among the likes of Ralph Lauren, Coach, Tommy Hilfiger, and Façonnable—describes it this way: branding used to be what you said about yourself, mostly in print. It then migrated to visual cues: icons, logos, packaging, and other forms of presentation that elevated and differentiated the attributes of what you sold from the alternatives. Branding molted from there into a statement about lifestyle, the idea that what you buy and who you do business with has the power to confirm your aspirational sense of yourself.

Then came a big shift. Rather than helping you imagine yourself as someone you hoped to be, branding rotated 180 degrees, to match who you already think you are. To capture you as you see yourself now, rather than advancing you as a mannequin for someone else. The greatest brands today reflect and touch deep with sincere understanding of the foundational psychology of the audiences they seek to attract; in personal and meaningful ways.

So what works today is the reverse of what most of us have grown up seeing as the formula for success. We've gone from building a business that helps people become something they hoped to be to building a business that understands and dignifies who they already are.

And how do you do this? Mike would say that it's by aligning your business's every touch with the outside world to the core values it sees in its intended audience. He would go on to say that the only way to pull this off is to first align the hearts and minds of everyone inside the company with those ideals. And that kind of alignment can arise and spread from only one source: the position at the top.

Your central role in the branding of your business is to be the Ralph Lauren, the Tommy Hilfiger, or the Pink of your organization. Others need to feel proud to be around you and imprint on your style and traits. This will build your business into a community with a clear persona that is conveyed consistently through every touch your business makes with the world around it. And it will attract like-minded people to support you, not just for what you sell them but for who you are.

# Chapter 10

## *Mission-Driven Business*

Chapter 3 made a brief reference to a different kind of business, one where the "atmosphere is electric." If you've ever felt the tingle of being in one, you know what I'm talking about and you've been astounded. These are businesses that vibrate with enthusiasm and positive impatience. The people who work there have bright eyes and wide smiles. They talk in machine-gun bursts that sound like secret code to outsiders and they walk fast with hands in a flurry. It can be disorienting to a visitor, who doesn't know how to get into the flow. As a visitor you stick out. But it looks so absorbing and inviting.

What brings that kind of energy to a company? And why isn't yours that way?

First question: What makes some companies so invigorating and appealing? People at these companies are striving together toward a goal that everyone feels is important, one that will make a big difference for others. And those involved will be proud to tell their kids and friends they helped to build the company and its brand. They see that, even though it might be a bold journey, the path ahead just might get the job done!

Everyone's got the spark in those companies. But there's only one place for it to start and to be kept alive, and that's at the top.

Only from the Job at the Top can this positive energy work down to the newest laborer and spread as a passion that spills over to customers, suppliers, the families of the people who come to work for you every day, and out into the communities you serve.

The second question is: Why isn't your business one of these high-energy companies? It could be. The only thing standing in the way...is **you!**

One of my favorite quotes is from Mahatma Gandhi, the great Indian thinker:

> *A man is but the product of his thoughts.*
> *What he thinks, he becomes.*

And Cross's corollary:

> *A business is but the product of the CEO's thoughts.*
> *What she thinks, it becomes.*

But what does it mean for you to think in a way that infects your whole business with a palpable zeal to get something important done?

Many years ago, when I asked one of my favorite mentors about his most valuable contributions as a CEO, he described quiet moments, after he'd spent time studying some aspect of his business, when an idea would come to him. Sometimes the idea about what his company might become seemed astounding, maybe even absurd, to someone without his perspective. It was always a long shot, but one that began looking more like a possibility as he continued to think. He'd continue to refine the idea and eventually distill it to a stirring proclamation of an outrageous mission.

> *By the third quarter of 20___, we shall become*
> _____!

Then, just as he would toss a smooth stone into a still pond, he would begin talking about his outrageous mission with his closest colleagues. Once they reached their own points of guarded confidence, he'd ask them to advocate with their own circles. And so on.

After a number of weeks, when everyone in the organization had been touched, something magical would happen. The culture would start to vibrate. And he would know then that his mission would be won.

So, how do you trigger the harmonics in your own company?

First, you have to think deeply about what your company might be able to become. Pick a time frame that's far enough out that there's time for something heroic to occur but close enough in to give the mission an edge. My favorite time frames fall in the six- to fifteen-month range.

This goal, then, becomes one of your focal points for your sixty minutes three times a week. Think without distraction about how to make your company vibrate. Shed the immediate restraints. And feel confident that when your idea is good enough you will find ways to take care of everything that stands in the way.

When your idea emerges, capture it in your own private draft statement of mission.

*By _____, we shall become _____!*

Then continue working on it. Let it simmer in your mind, examining and refining every word until you become obsessed as the inaugural believer—until you understand that it just might be possible. The acid test is when your idea walks the knife's edge between the truly absurd and what just might be possible. The time to reveal it is when you can't shake your thoughts of making it happen.

At that point, start discussing it with your closest allies, over several conversations. Take in their reactions and adjust your idea as appropriate, then ask them to do the same with their teams. Continue until everyone in your business is touched. Review the reactions.

Then, start talking about your mission incessantly, with everyone. Weave it into every communication. Applaud those who've made contributions toward its achievement and encourage those who haven't.

And you? You'll find new depth, fascination, and love for your Job at the Top, because you'll be doing it well and achieving the mission you have created.

# Chapter 11

## *Establishing Loyalty*

The two best ways to endear your business to customers are to help them over a fear or to make them feel better about themselves. Today, more than ever before, these two tactics are your highest-voltage power tools for brand support and a continually vibrant top line.

Just think about it. What is it that makes you choose one dry cleaner over another? My hunch? It's because the business you prefer has gotten you over a fear that your favorite suit or dress might not be ready when you need it for that big meeting or cocktail party. Or the cleaner has assuaged your worry that your prized wardrobe piece might be damaged when it's out of your possession. Something as simple as the clerk commenting on the great quality of the dress you're handing over or remembering to ask about how you felt in the jacket at the party separates this dry cleaner by miles from the one with the clerk who presents the receipt without ever looking up.

What makes you buy your clothes, home furnishings, or cars from one vendor rather than another? My hunch here is similar, but in this area it's less about getting someone over a fear than it is about making that person feel great about himself—by making him feel attractive, smart, powerful, successful, or appreciated.

But this approach... of matching the experience your business delivers to the things your customers care about most, whether those are directly related, tangentially related, or unrelated to what you actually sell…is not yet popular among marketers or businesspeople because it involves right-brain thinking. It's not logical and neatly measurable. It's also contrary to nearly everything that's made them successful in the past. But societal patterns and cultural norms are changing, and they're changing fast. Given our immediate access to everything we want to know and the realities of our "new normal" global economy, business as usual is passing away. In its wake is rising a business environment in which the specific attributes of what people buy are less meaningful in their purchasing decisions than the experiences they have when buying.

So, what does this mean for the person in the Job at the Top? It means rethinking every aspect of your business according to new standards. Sure, you've got to continue offering great products and services. But that is no longer sufficient. Wrapped around *what you sell* must be your obsession with *what it feels like* to do business with you, whether you are helping customers over their fears or helping them feel better about themselves.

This means new focal points for your attention. Sure, you still need to be forcefully committed to the competitive specifics of your offerings, and you need to be on constant alert for ways to improve what you provide. But other considerations—many of them only indirectly related to what you actually sell, like your interest in helping your customers over a hidden fear or making them feel better about themselves—have likely slipped into the rationale that is driving customers to your door. Or, perhaps, to someone else's.

Do you ever find yourself wondering why your customer base and your top line have eroded? They've slipped even though you've added new items, increased your marketing efforts, and lowered prices. Despite the economic situation, most of the customers you've lost are still buying from someone; the likelihood is high that they've gone to someone who is better attuned to the emotional content of the relationship they seek than you are.

At a nationwide automobile collision repair franchise, CARSTAR, which I took over in insolvency, the top line turned up dramatically the moment we stopped thinking about our business as fixing dents and paint and started thinking of it as a business that helped people get through crises in their lives. This business was about how people could get their kids to school, avoid being shortchanged by their insurance companies, and find someone to teach their teenagers to be safe, accident-free drivers. In three years we doubled the franchise base, generated significant earnings, and sold the company for an outstanding multiple of past earnings.

How did we accomplish such a dramatic turnaround? Simply by understanding what was really on the minds of our customers and reorienting the business to calm their fears and help them feel better about themselves at a time of uncertainty.

Back to our dry cleaning example: my own choice of dry cleaner has nothing to do with the quality or the price of cleaning. All of the local dry cleaning establishments offer about the same level of quality and cost. My preference for Patriot Cleaners has everything to do with a friendly counter person; with the fresh, high-quality coffee at the ready; with a pleasant place to sit and chat about town issues; with an owner who's well informed; and with a staff that has the zeal to rush a job and deliver to my home if I need it. This is a business my friends support, and one that supports charities I admire. If those aspects of the customer experience changed, so would my choice.

Into your sixty-minute sessions, add time spent answering the following question: How can you make your business as important to your customers as Patriot Cleaners is to me? How can you make it as distinguished as CARSTAR is in the markets it serves?

# Chapter 12

## *Revelation: The Answers Aren't in the Numbers*

In chapter 8, I talked about the obsession with "the numbers" that exploded in the 1960s, when the new "science" of decision theory crossed paths with low-cost computer power. At that moment, business scholars began the stampede toward a new "law": *given enough numbers, anyone can run anything.*

Quickly, business became more about math than about the understanding of emotion, behavior, and relationships in commerce. It became more about logic than about judgment.

Now that pendulum is swinging back. And, as happens with most cultural swings, being out in front (but not too far) is a position of advantage for a leader in the Job at the Top.

There are three things you need to know:

• Even the toughest financial zealots are beginning to realize that there's more to running a successful business than spreadsheets. Too many Excel-justified loans have failed. Too many overanalyzed investments in private equity and venture portfolios have disappointed. Most business leaders are now realizing that in order to make money, you actually have to make a business better. You can't just sustain, refinance, or model it.

•   Still, you can't ignore the numbers game. There is good in it; the financials serve as an indicator for how well everything else is going for your business. Moreover, much of our financial infrastructure still underpins our access to capital and banking relations. Additionally, the formulas that determine the values of our businesses are important forces to consider.

•   Even though these numbers constitute the scorecard for most of the world of finance, they are not necessarily the best objective function for delivering exceptional results. In your own world, in your Job at the Top, you can think differently. The Back of the Envelope and the other frameworks provided in this book— as well as additional examples outlined in *Just Run It!*—will help you form your thoughts about what your business needs to be and how to get it there, *before* turning to the arithmetic. After you reach these conclusions, you can use the numbers to verify your projections.

What is the role of financial modeling, then? It tests and calibrates, rather than discovers, what's best for your business. Discovery is your responsibility. And that treasure is not found on spreadsheets.

So, what does this mean for actually performing your Job at the Top?

It means you need to assume responsibility as the Head Thinker and the Head Mathematician. Your field of view must be broad and deep. You need to spend most of your time gathering and synthesizing information about how the pieces of your business fit together and about how well your business fits in with the environmental changes around it. Then you should use the numbers to check your thinking and to help you identify opportunities to improve. Defaulting to a focus on the numbers as your initial evaluative tool is a tempting slide, because it seems easier than unstructured, projective thinking, and because numbers are the language you use with your bankers and investors.

But I guarantee that looking at the numbers won't get you out of most jams. Only thinking will.

The kind of deep thinking that will improve your business requires that you spend more time in the company of customers, knowledgeable observers, other smart businesspeople, trend watchers, and technologists. It means spending your sixty minutes alone three days a week. And it means discussing your thinking with a small circle of trusted co-thinkers, and together looking for the patterns and big ideas that will transform your business into something extraordinary. You should engage others in the later stages of your conclusions, rather than bringing them in at your early musings.

Then and only then, after you have done your thinking, turn to the arithmetic to vet your conclusions.

## Deeper Thinking

- Form a breakfast group—schedule a weekly or biweekly gathering of good thinkers to discuss business issues.
- Teach—offer a course at a local college or prep school in business management.
- Join associations—become active in your industry association.
- Read—reserve time every day for thought-provoking reading.
- Avoid television—use the time you gain more productively, for the other pursuits on this list or for relaxing or personal enrichment.
- Take notes—keep a special notebook of key thoughts of the day and review it weekly.

# Chapter 13

## *The Magic of Renewal*

Chapter 5 introduced Bruce Henderson's product life cycle concept, which hit business thinking in the 1970s with the force of an atomic blast.

Today we're seeing more, and more frequent, exceptions to the natural and "inevitable" progression of businesses from the embryonic through growth, maturing, and aging and decline stages that Henderson espoused. Increasingly, we're seeing examples that defy that "law" of nature—and when they do, they continually leave others roiling in their wake. These innovative businesses furrow the brows of those in the Jobs at the Top at rivals that can't keep pace, as they wonder how to run their own businesses that well.

Twenty years ago I began advocating an alternative to the life cycle, a different way to consider, particularly, the inevitable decline and ending posited by the life cycle model.

In the life cycle model, the frogs that have made it from eggs (the embryonic stage) through tadpoles (the growth stage) are destined to age and slow down, until they slip off the lily pad and settle into the detritus at the bottom of the pond. In my Renewal Model, there's the possibility for vigorous frogs at the growth stage to leap across a Gray Zone into new positions on the lower ranges of a new cycle; from there they can move up, then leap again.

That's exactly what the most vibrant businesses do these days, but few of us understand how.

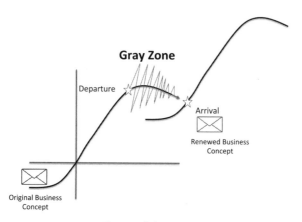

*Renewal diagram*

The path we are talking about is the one I've designated with the oscillating line on the diagram, which connects a takeoff point from the mature range of the curve, on the left, to a landing spot at a lower point on the growth range of a new curve to the right. This bouncing line depicts redefining the business; it's a path that carries forward the parts that are still relevant but leaves behind those that aren't, and adds in others that convolve the business into a new whole with solid growth opportunity ahead. The swings in amplitude of the line emphasize that "curve jumping" is never a straightforward, business-as-usual exercise. It's experimental, disruptive, risky, and takes a big leap of faith on the part of everyone involved.

This is a journey that's not a fit for everyone, for two reasons:

First, because most businesses wait too long before deciding to try…they wait until declining performance through the maturity stage has depleted financial resources below the levels required to endure the trip. Here, as with a lot of things, early detection and decisive action pay off. It's far better to make the decision to jump curves when confidence in the business is strong and its war chest is full, before it proceeds too deeply into maturity. As a piece of logic, this advice is compelling. But rare is the management team with the foresight and the courage to depart from a solidly performing business and set sail for another, better alternative.

Second, curve jumping isn't an exercise for the timid nor for set-in-their-ways types. It requires a maniacally optimistic spirit of adventure, which represents a 180-degree flip from what works in the Job at the Top in the mature stage. It's night and day. Black and white. Back toward what worked in the Job at the Top during the embryonic stage, but with a big multiplier. Starting a business, as we noted in chapter 6, is the stuff of charismatic leadership, which can be surficial. Moving an organization and its people, who have settled into the routines of running a mature business, off their stable base... to take a chance at reconfiguring onto a better one... is the deeper stuff of "Braveheart" obsession and influence!

What prevents more of us from becoming "Bravehearts" and driving our businesses through continual renewals rather than into the mud at the bottom of the pond? It's an ancient nemesis: the allure of the known versus the risks of the unknown.

It takes courage to even consider stepping off a still-floating ship, even if we sense that its day has passed. It's scary to venture off in a small whaleboat to find a better land. (For a riveting account of just such an experience, read *Endeavor*, an account of Captain Ernest Shackleton's yearlong journey in a whaleboat launched from a foundered mother ship across the ice-bound Antarctic seas at the South Pole.) So, what does it take to be an explorer, like Shackleton, rather than a deteriorating old frog in your Job at the Top?

The answer? Dissatisfaction!

## Eternal Frogs

- Ford Motor Company reinvented itself at the brink of disaster with a call to action on product competitiveness.
- Apple Computer superseded its own products as soon as competitors caught up.
- USAA diversified from personal insurance for military officers to full financial services for all.
- Hyundai and Kia transformed from producing cheap imports to supplying high-quality, high-performance luxury vehicles.
- Ralph Lauren expanded its lines to include Polo, Polo Sport, Polo Kids, Polo Home Furnishings, Lauren, and Purple Label.

Dissatisfaction is not to be confused with unhappiness; in fact, it's just the opposite. You need to be consumed with the positive energy that comes from seeing an opportunity to experience something far better than what you're experiencing now. Being dissatisfied means never being beguiled into complacency with the status quo, never being on cruise control. Instead, you're driving your organization at speeds considered reckless by onlookers. You are carrying forward the best of what got you to where you are and shedding no tears about leaving behind what's no longer relevant. You are amazing people with what you become next. And next. And next.

How do you do that? Let's go back to the basics. You do it by protecting at all costs your position as the Head Thinker—for sixty minutes three days a week. You work at it every week, including the weeks of gravest crisis, because the excitement you release with your zeal about what might lie around the next bend is what's most likely going to get you successfully around that next bend.

Start taking some time in your sessions to imagine what might lie just around the bend. Think about what your business could be. You'll likely surprise yourself with what might happen!

## The Best Around-the-Bend Exercise

Every Monday morning write down three things you wish were different about your business. Tape the list to your wall where you can't avoid seein g it. If you really care about making those changes, you will. Or you'll simply drop the exercise. Which will it be?

# Chapter 14

## *Kill Your Culture*

Protecting your position as Head Thinker—committing to your sixty-minute sessions three days a week—is critical to running your company well. But it's not sufficient. In order to carry your organization along with you, there's something more to your job. And that is releasing your followers to be astronauts, too. You need to break the bonds that hold your colleagues back, which in most organizations is a considerable task.

How do you unlock widespread passion for adventure? In most organizations it means killing a part of your culture. The difficulty is that our legacy concepts of organizational structure and control are anchored in beliefs that people aren't smart enough or motivated enough to do what's best for the business on their own. The residue of those beliefs fosters conservatism and replaces the spirit of adventure with the fear of being wrong.

So there's danger in getting yourself all worked up in your sixty-minute sessions every week if others don't get worked up too. If you're the only soul infected with the adventure bug, you'll be setting yourself up for a futile exercise, a one-man Pickett's Charge. Without colleagues to strike out for new territory along with you, you'll be alone out in front while everyone else hides behind the rock wall of the practices that have provided safety in the past. Many of us have seen this play out before. And some of us have done it!

Fear of the unknown, linked with fear of failure, is why most people in Jobs at the Top seldom give heroic things even a moment of serious thought. Instead, they hunker down behind the stone walls with everyone else.

What a regrettable circumstance!

How do you break away from the malaise of timidity? How do you create a culture that vibrates with guts and verve? It's not too difficult, nor does it take long—*if* you've got the guts and verve to make it happen.

It all depends on you. On your willingness to forgo your own safety chute, and on your willingness to take risks and support others who travel the path with you, both when they're right and when they're wrong.

Where's the best place to start? Begin with something seen as risky, but that has low potential for damage. What that project is depends entirely upon you. Examples I've used include things like developing a short-term promotional program for a specific product or service, rethinking and then testing an amended administrative or production process, or asking someone else to lead a meeting that you've customarily led. Even cold-calling a prime account with which you've had no previous business can make a great deal of difference.

## A Good Place to Start

At MW Manufacturers, we started our move toward lean manufacturing in an isolated, small, self-contained production cell that made a not-too-important product. Without fanfare we began teaching and implementing lean ideas and practices. The effects on productivity and morale were outstanding. Soon, word leaked out and everyone wanted her department to be next.

Let people know what you're about to try, and tell them you're not certain of the result. Though this is counterintuitive, the best outcome will be that your endeavor is not entirely successful. If that happens, ask for help in understanding what went wrong, then try again. Hopefully, one of your efforts will lead to success. If it doesn't, admit a false start, recalibrate the objective, and repeat the sequence. Then start encouraging a few others to do likewise. Return the courtesy of thoughtful support when they fail.

Generally, this process of seeing you take risks and survive the trial kills the attitude of "do it my way and get the right result, or you're in trouble" and starts replacing it with "you'll never be in trouble for trying to improve the company within the generally accepted boundaries of responsible initiative."

And when those conservative tendencies are gone, you're ready to take a bigger jump. You're prepared to defy the natural law of the frogs, with confidence that your organization is behind you.

This is fun stuff to think about in your sixty minutes three days a week.

# Chapter 15

## *Eastern Versus Western Medicine for Business*

A forceful undercurrent of thinking is gaining momentum in Western medicine. It has nothing to do with politics or funding; it's about our baseline approach to restoring and maintaining health. This movement weighs the benefits of Eastern versus Western philosophy, and its effects are starting to spill over into business.

Our Western approach to problem solving—a style so pervasive that we don't even question its validity—isn't natural law. Sir Isaac Newton charted a path for new discoveries in physics, astronomy, and mathematics. His breakthrough scientific method changed the way humans looked at problems, and has set the pattern for Western thinking ever since.

Until now, that is. Leading medical minds are now considering the unfathomable: that Newton may have been wrong!

Newton's scientific method disaggregated complex things into their component parts, presuming that if the parts could be understood, the whole could be understood. That kind of thinking is why business schools offer twenty-six courses on the subparts of a business. It's also why, if you ask someone a question about the whole of business, such as *"How do you run a business?"* the response will likely be a blank stare. We are conditioned to think like Newton, from the parts up rather than from the whole down. Eastern philosophy works the other way around. Eastern thinkers start with a broad theory of a healthy whole, and then seek to understand the relationships of all the influences—on the inside, on the outside, and between the two—in diagnosing discontinuities.

So, how does this way of thinking translate into running a business? How is it relevant to those of us who have Jobs at the Top?

## Eastern Thinking Transforms Building Products

Since 1938 MW had been a regional manufacturer of residential windows and doors with a product line that offered "Andersen quality" at costs that didn't need to cover national advertising. Placement with local building supply had been based on keeping pace with Andersen improvements. Upon takeover, we began looking at MW holistically and soon concluded that the Andersen quality was only part of what the business was all about. On-time and complete delivery of easy-to-install units often made or broke the profitability of individual building projects. Industry-wide, performance on these expectations was low. A complete reconfiguration of the business to ensure 100 percent on-time delivery with installation support drove this regional player from an unknown to a national award winner and a gain on sale of $80 million.

Applying these tenets of Eastern philosophy to businesses reinforces the importance of reserving time in our sixty-minute sessions to focus our thinking about our business as a whole rather than as a collection of parts. We need to view our businesses as continuously evolving, integrated systems of forces and processes that relate to one another in dynamic and complex ways. When we stop and do this, we recognize that shifts in one area reverberate through all the others. The shifts may be positive in nature or they may be negative. And the best actions to take are often counterintuitive. The most obvious target for a key solution might not actually be the right move. A sharp decline in sales, for example, might have little to do with your sales organization, its leadership, or the incentive system, but rather be rooted in the emergence of an alternative technology or a shift in tastes that you've missed. Tinkering with the subparts of the sales system will never have the desired effect. Only when you look at the whole of the phenomenon of the decline will you be likely to find the true solution.

The solution may be something you've never even thought about before.

From the Eastern perspective, our Job at the Top isn't about fixing parts. It's about maintaining a balanced and vigorous whole. We can help do this by focusing more on the interactions of elements that add or reduce friction in moving toward our intended futures.

In the Eastern model, our Job at the Top requires a more open field of view than the current month's, quarter's, and year's financials, chunked down through independent metrics to evaluations of separate departments' and individuals' performance.

When you dig a little deeper, you find that the businesses we admire most today are led in the Eastern way by individuals who have the capacity to integrate an array of signals into a pattern of the whole that others don't see. These leaders must also have the discipline to stay intensely focused on the whole and the courage to act upon what they believe is right. As a result, these leaders are the destinies of their companies.

Leading-edge thinkers in medicine are predicting that, fifty years from now, medical schools will be restructured to concentrate on what they call *functional physicians*. These doctors look at the whole of an individual's life to understand the broader patterns that lead to health. Rather than being looked down on as "only generalists," they'll be practicing at the vanguard of medical care. Eventually, we'll stop treating patients as collections of independent problems and treat them instead as the beautiful, not necessarily entirely predictable and logical, wholes that they are.

So, if this approach works for people—as it seems to work for people in the East—why shouldn't it also work for businesses in the West?

Think about it, explicitly, for sixty minutes three days a week.

# Chapter 16

## *Activity Beats Execution*

The execution fads in business—just like strategic planning, management by objective, total quality, just-in-time, and other methods before these—have had their day. In their wake, these fads have left a predictable legacy of unproductive time and talk, as well as failed expectations.

Like most fashionable concepts of their decades, execution really hasn't made much difference. Mainly, it's hung a new title on something we've known all along that we need to do: move our organizations forward.

The problem with much execution thinking lies in its presumption about the way organizations advance. The execution movement sees organizational advance as a sequence of assaults, each with its own independent targets, plans to apply resources, metrics to track progress, enforcing mechanisms, and independent ends. Collectively, these efforts are supposed to achieve the previously articulated, measurable, and overarching goals of the organization.

This approach is derived from Newton's idea that, in order to make something big happen, we have to break it down into its component parts and concentrate on those. Usually, one or more bad things happens in these kinds of exercises: the breakdown of components is misconceived; a few or a lot of the small initiatives fail; or all the initiatives work but they don't deliver the overarching intention.

The through line of most truly vibrant businesses isn't a series of independent, and not necessarily well coordinated, assaults toward a predetermined, long-range, and vaguely defined target. These companies' paths are, instead, more like our own lives: a continuous unfolding of experiences, understandings, adjustments, and progress, with plenty of improvisation along the way.

So how, from your position of responsibility at the top, can you mobilize this kind of holistic, organic unfolding? The great news is that it's more about simply letting it happen than forcing anything to occur. Your role is to unlock organizational ingenuity—the kind of ingenuity that engages and aligns the whole of your company's brainpower and enthusiasm—in activities that move it forward along a continuously unfolding path. And, once that momentum is initiated, to offer counsel and guidance. Your job is not setting every target, monitoring the efforts, and looking for the shortfalls of every plan. Rather, it is to be clear about your intentions and about the boundaries of appropriate innovation.

You should invite everyone to step forward.

## Unlocking Whole-Business Ingenuity

- Host "Brainstorming with the CEO," periodic cross-functional and vertically mixed discussions on "What Could Our Business Be?"
- Invite and reward paragraphs of the month, employee writings on "Our Business 36 Months from Now," to be posted in the monthly newsletter.
- Hold off-site gatherings with your executive team to develop a list of "tangible images" for your business future twelve to thirty-six months out.
- Once a year, invite employees to submit characterizations of their ideal circumstances at work—which I call Personal Perfection. Distribute the results and include actions the

business will be able to take toward those goals within a reasonable time horizon. Also include explanations of those actions it can't take, because of limited resources for investment, systems constraints, fairness, and the like.

---

How, more specifically, do you initiate this momentum? You need to swap out rigid schedules of tasks with rigid deadlines, for more flexible milestones that lay out a path for learning how to make the whole organization operate more effectively and enthusiastically.

But there's a preamble: it's your compelling idea about what your company might become, if you try. This preamble emerges from your thinking alone, sixty minutes three days a week.

I usually frame this preamble as a certain achievement in a time period of nine to twenty months, depending on the nature and complexity of the goal. I lay out what look to me like reasonable, interim milestones—the things we need to learn and adjust about how we operate in order to achieve the goal. Then I engage teams to begin thinking about what it's going to take to achieve each milestone. Finally, I provide constructive encouragement and oversight that transfers the findings and advances from each team to the thinkers on the other teams. Eventually, we meet to commit to the decisions and actions that will achieve the results.

A contrast of examples helps:

### Execution–Deadline Thinking

Goal: Grow profits for June 30 by 15%
Plan:

> Introduce new product X by time Y
> Reduce raw materials costs by Z%
> Upgrade the sales manager and add two reps in
>     60 days
> Hire a branding consultant
> Redesign the website in Q2

Launch a social media campaign for Q3
*Sound familiar?*

### Learning–Milestone Thinking

Compelling idea: Take over #1 position in our business
over 1–2 years
Path:

Learn from customers why we're #3, Q1

Develop a list of possible adjustments, Q1–2

Test sets of adjustments on customer behavior and
evaluate responses by rivals #1 and #2, Q2–3

Refine understanding of timing, costs, and risks of
the best alternatives, Q4

Launch one or more initiatives, Q4–1

Monitor and adjust initiatives as we move forward,
Q1–4

Execution–Deadline thinking is anchored in the notion that we
can identify meaningful, long-term objectives and define the specific actions that will achieve those objectives at the outset, before
we even get started. It assumes we can act with military rigidity
and ensure compliance. It also presupposes that compliance will
achieve our goal.

Learning–Milestone thinking acknowledges the likelihood
of discovery along the way and recognizes that the target and the
means of its attainment may change based on those new findings.
The Learning–Milestone approach allows for improvisational
fluidity and invites you to revisit for yourself, during your sixty-
minute sessions, your company's evolving targets and the methods
you'll use to hit them. It also offers a useful way for you to start
discussing your thoughts with others, who will inspire creativity
throughout your organization and help your company reach a level
of vibrancy that Execution–Deadline thinking never achieves!

# Chapter 17

## *Your Goggles for Greatness*

We've noted the problem...no one talks about the whole of our Jobs at the Top. Particularly, no one talks about what we need to do to move our businesses forward as a whole, quickly and profitably.

This chapter introduces a framework that puts all the relevant perspectives for making that happen in place. And it's a framework that works. This is my short version on how to move your business from average to great, and it has never let me down. Admittedly, you'll find here only the headlines, the rough agenda for your consideration—we'll dig deeper later. But simply having this framework in mind will get you thinking more clearly about the whole of your Job at the Top, right now.

Here's the logic.

Businesses arise because someone has an idea that generates revenues sufficient to cover the costs. From there, success depends on our cleverness in looking through our close-in lenses and perfecting *execution*.

But eventually, even highly perfected execution yields declining results, due to the effects of new competition, changing customer tastes, costs that rise faster than prices, new technology, and/or regulation. Regardless of how well we execute, eventually all our original business ideas must change. Or fail.

Shifting your attention from the inside—through your close-in lens of *execution*—to the outside—through your mid-range lens of *strategy,* you begin to look over the walls. You need to look to the outside to see what your business needs to become, and how to make the change.

But as solid as your new strategy may be, shifting out of existing and entrenched patterns of day-to-day execution isn't easy. There's natural friction between the "now"—how things are currently done, which proved successful in the past—and the "future"—how things need to be done in order to deliver on the new strategy.

Shifting your field of view again to your third and longest-range lens for *vision* is how you bridge that gap.

Great vision brings four other perspectives on your business into focus for everyone. These four perspectives, led and protected from the top, are what fill an organization with a spirit of adventure, nobility, and confidence to move forward decisively and aggressively.

The first of these is a simple but compelling set of core values. These ideas are the "sacred yardstick" for measuring the appropriateness of every decision in the business. Just three or four ideals stated in as few words as possible are what you are seeking; they must be short enough, simple enough, and meaningful enough that everyone can remember them.

The second component of effective vision is a clear statement of purpose: why the world is a better place because of your business. Again, it should be a short, unambiguous, and emotionally gripping statement about the "higher calling" of your business. The best statements of purpose convey an intention that never will be fully accomplished, but that ennobles everyone in its pursuit.

In combination, compelling core values and an inspiring statement of purpose constitute what I call the "DNA" of your business. These are the fundamental concepts that underpin the character of your business and which people can count on being preserved from one stage of the life cycle to the next as well as from business curve to curve.

The third of the four components is an electrifying statement of mission. In chapter 10 we described the differences between businesses that are mission-driven and those that aren't; the chief difference is an atmosphere of energy and passion. What lies at the core of those emotions is a widely shared commitment to accomplish something extraordinary. The best statements of mission "walk the knife's edge" between what outsiders might see as an absurd intention but which those on the inside believe just might be attainable.

The fourth and final component of effective vision is a collection of highly aspirational mental images of what life in your business will be like for everyone who is a part of it when your mission is accomplished—I call these "tangible images."

Once you've brought the trifocal Goggles for Greatness into your business and taught everyone to see through the lenses, you will witness amazing forces emerge in your organization. First, the general level of enthusiasm and morale will rise. Next, you'll see relevant ideas for how to move your business forward emerging from every corner. And third, you'll realize that what you have put in place has the potential to be a new and perpetual "pacemaker" that speeds up the heart of your enterprise.

Think about how to do this explicitly—about how to keep the energy and passion going through your own activities and behavior—in your sixty minutes three days a week.

---

## Battery Solutions' Vision

Following are the core values, purpose, mission statement, and tangible images of Battery Solutions, the largest recycler of battery chemistries in the United States.

Core Values:
  At BSL we believe deeply in:
    Truth
    Transparency
    Fairness
    Passion for our service
Purpose:
  BSL exists to:
    Protect people and places
Mission:
  By year end 2013:
    We shall put in place the platform to double
      our business in 2015–2016
Tangible Images:
  At year end 2015 we shall enjoy:
    Full-service battery solutions
    National brand
    Exceptional rewards
    Paths for advancement
    Charitable works
    Culture of zeal

---

Maintaining your organization's understanding of the balance between vision, strategy, and execution is your job. Continually reinforced through your actions, it keeps your organization confident and moving forward. Your job is setting the pace for others and filling your organization with anticipation for what's coming next.

# Chapter 18

## *Strategy and Execution*

I still carry the sting of seeing the cover of a leading business magazine, which stopped me dead in my tracks as I was hustling down an airport concourse in the early 1990s. It changed my life's work. Big black letters on a blood red background read: *Strategy Didn't Work!*

Hurriedly scratching past the ads to find the lead article, I locked in on a chart that compared strategic planning expenditures with business performance to show convincingly that there was no positive correlation! All other thoughts receded.

I was dumbstruck. Because, somewhere in my consciousness, I'd known the judgment was right. And because I'd spent a decade establishing myself as a strategic planning expert.

In that very moment in Boston Logan's Concourse C, I understood a painfully humbling truth. I'd consumed way too much in clients' funds creating beautiful and unassailable strategic plans, which were memorialized in thick, fancy, three-ring binders. But they seldom made any difference.

It's not that the plans were wrong. They would have worked, and with devastating effectiveness! The trouble was that my team and I were the only ones who understood the plans well enough to commit to their execution.

Sure, sometimes we'd get solid buy-in from a CEO and a few

members of the executive team. But that wasn't enough to over-come the rest of their organization's reluctance to change things.

It took quite some deliberation and time for me to come up with an alternative approach that worked. But eventually I did. The result? My "plans" are now no more than five short bullets—each fewer than eight words—which I write on one side of an index card. That's it!

And what's so effective about this almost embarrassingly minimalist approach to strategy, compared with the evidentiary-quality binders? A blindingly smart CEO on the West Coast crys-tallized it for me: "Dick, if you can't get it down to forty words on one side of an index card...you just haven't thought about it hard enough!"

The beauty of the Index Card Strategy is that everyone can understand the whole scheme. They can also see how the initia-tives work together and reinforce one another, and they can imag-ine in totality how the company might be different and better when the plan is in place. They can remember it. And they can begin to think on their own about how to contribute to the plan's realization.

The question remains: "How do you come up with the three, four, or five ideas, and what qualifies as a strategy?"

The linchpin is in the statement of mission you craft as part of your vision for your business and then promote with unceas-ing passion. This is the idea we talked about in chapters 10 and 17, the one that walks the knife's edge between what's absurd even to think about and what just might be possible.

Your mission is the next heroic objective that you have con-vinced yourself and everyone else is an exciting possibility—clearly a stretch but nonetheless an enticing potential—for your business. Remember, it has a timeline that is far enough out to be an eye-popping accomplishment but close enough in to have an edge. The Index Card Strategy, then, simply outlines the handful of hurdles you need to clear in order to move from your current reality to the realization of that mission.

People often confuse the mission with the things they need to do in order to keep the business, as it is currently configured, healthy and moving forward. Those things don't qualify. Strategies are different. They're bigger. Strategies are the things that will transform your business into something better than it is today.

Strategies include things like implanting yourself in the preferences of new categories of customers. They include changing or broadening your offering to address new and compelling needs; reconstructing how you are known to match a more vibrant market opportunity; developing a technology that others won't be able to match; and, usually, adding new competencies and discontinuing others as your new business model takes over.

In fact, strategies are things that change your Back of the Envelope business concept, which we talked about in chapter 7. Lesser actions that don't change the fundamental logic of your Back of the Envelope are improvements, not strategies.

Once you've settled on a set of five or fewer strategies that you believe will rewrite your Back of the Envelope and carry you to your mission, your final and determining step, execution, becomes a lot easier. It's easier to plan and budget, and easier for everyone to understand.

Execution at that point is simply the collection of mini-plans that correspond to each strategy. You'll have three, four, or five strategies and three, four, or five execution plans. That's it. No binder!

Of course, there are feedback loops. You may find out, for example, that the execution plans for a particular strategy are beyond your technical means or that you don't have the financial resources to support the investment at this time. Simple. Go back, re-specify your strategies, and try again.

It's unfortunate that the black eye strategy suffered in the

1970s, '80s, and '90s has turned so many people in Jobs at the Top entirely away from the idea. Don't be one of those. Electrify your organization with a simple and compelling set of strategies and execution plans linked directly to a noble and deeply inspiring mission. That's your job and no one else's.

---

## Mission and Strategy at Battery Solutions

Mission:
　By year-end 2013:
　We shall put in place the platform to double
　　　our business in 2015–2016
Strategy:
- Build an enterprise-level sales organization
- Achieve highest environmental certifications
- Expand service and geographic footprint

---

# Chapter 19

## *The Team Trap*

I horrified an audience recently when I called teamwork *the greatest drain on contemporary business productivity.* And it's likely that I've just had the same effect on you!

It's not that the idea of team is fundamentally bad. It's wonderful... in situations where more than one mind or body is required to create an outcome. The troubles come when we use teams in situations where they're not necessary.

Teamwork has become a universal default for dealing with far too many things. Often, it just slows down our processes, reduces decisions to least-common-denominator solutions, raises risk aversion, and undermines responsibility and accountability.

In some businesses the trend has grown to epidemic proportions, with individuals feeling slighted if they're not included in proceedings that fall far from their own range of responsibilities and beyond their abilities to contribute. The consequence is that no one takes personal responsibility—which isn't a euphemism for punishment, but rather a focus on high-impact learning—when things go wrong.

How often have you asked, *"What went wrong?"* or *"Is this the best we can do?"* to receive an answer that started with, *"Well, when the team..."*

The point here isn't to ascribe blame but rather to accelerate the momentum of your business. Personal responsibility encourages employees to become stronger by learning from their successes and their failures—as individuals.

Shelves in the business sections of book vendors and listings online are replete with advice on team building. A consistent takeaway from this considerable literature is the observation that teams are only as strong as the strengths of their members. Without discounting the truth that solid teams improve the contributions of their individual members, it's important to acknowledge that weak members hold teams back. Teams of strong members become productivity multipliers, given situations that warrant teamwork.

So, getting the best out of teams and avoiding the negatives starts with every individual accepting the responsibility that she needs to be better. As Mary Baker Eddy, one of my favorite nineteenth-century thinkers, wrote, "*O make me glad for every scalding tear.*"

Great and strong businesses and great and strong teams are collections of great and strong individuals. They're like an army. They are made up of individuals who have, first, stood on their own and have been tested. But these are also people who have the capacity to come together and shoulder the weight of reaching a complicated goal as a team. And they do this without abdicating their responsibility as individuals to every other individual and without abdicating their individual responsibility to contribute to the success of the whole.

And that's where you come in, from your position in the Job at the Top. Here are a few suggestions to ensure that your teams are used efficiently and effectively.

- Only mobilize a team when an objective warrants multiple perspectives.
- Only staff a team with members whose experiences will add meaningfully to the outcome.

- Set unambiguous objectives and clear end points.
- Evaluate the contributions of members along the way, with debriefing at the end.
- Finally, leave other initiatives to individuals according to the scopes of their organizational responsibilities.

And a final note: your own position is not a team job. People say, "It's lonely at the top" for a reason. Your job is to think and act at a level different from everyone else. You may seek counsel, but you can never abdicate your responsibility for the health and integrity of your whole business.

Demonstrate this, and expect it from others, and you'll begin to discern in your sixty-minute sessions the right times and the right balance in your business for individual and team contributions.

# Chapter 20

## *To Tweet or Not to Tweet*

A lot of us tweet, blog, watch our websites, and monitor Facebook. But I know few CEOs who have actually absorbed the full impact of social media into their thinking about running their businesses. To some of us, social media still feels a little disconnected. It's like something we've added to our closet, but it's not an exact fit with the rest of our wardrobe.

Stay with me for the next three and a half minutes, and we'll begin to move through that fog together!

Viewing social media as something you've got to do because others, particularly younger people, do it misses the point. The challenge for us in our Jobs at the Top isn't a matter of learning how to do it. Our challenge is understanding what social media means for our businesses. It's recognizing how the new era of communication changes our relationships, mainly with our customers but also with everyone else. The new connectedness changes how people think, and it changes what they expect from us in order to continue to support us and give us their business.

For as long as we can remember, the drivers of customer buying behavior have been functions, features, quality, price, service, and convenience. If you could win on these fronts, you'd have the business. But social media has made that prescription obsolete. And that's the big point—the mega message—we need to accept.

Social media has leveled the traditional bases of competition—functions, features, quality, and so on. With a tap on a phone or tablet screen, customers now connect with more sellers of products and services than they ever knew existed, accessing offerings that are likely to be easily substituted for ours, in their estimation.

At the same time, social media has spawned communities of interest on nearly every imaginable topic. Customers and other interested parties can now share unbiased and independent opinions about one provider's virtues compared with another's. And these people's views have huge impacts on the opinions and choices of today's consumers.

So, the short and sweet version is: today, your customers have far more choices that compare favorably with your offering than ever before. And they can communicate instantaneously with others about their real-life experiences with you and your rivals. Today, there's full exposure of you and your competitors.

So, what does this shift mean for you in your Job at the Top? It means rethinking your business, starting with what you need to stand for in order to remain relevant. It means accepting that what made your business competitive in the past—the features, functions, quality, price, service, and convenience of your products—is no longer sufficient. And it means that you may have to pay more attention to, and perhaps even reconfigure, how you are seen through the lens of social media by your customers. You may need to include things that never entered into your thinking before, like the charities and social causes you support. Or you might highlight what's special about your workforce, key elements of your company culture, the kinds of things you reward, or the extra lengths to which you go to ensure consistent and responsible care of the environment, your employees' families, your suppliers, and your industry. These are things that will keep customers supporting you and will encourage others to give you a try.

From your customers' end of the microscope, access to comparable options for most goods and services logically leads them to shift their bases for making buying decisions to these kinds of higher planes of preference. Increasingly, customers are looking beyond what you actually sell and zeroing in on what it's like to do business with you. They're responding to the persona of your business and to *who they like most and, therefore, want to "gift" with their business!*

How do you win on these terms? First, you have to maintain your competitiveness on all the other dimensions—features, functions, quality, price, service, and convenience. But with all that pretty much expected now, you need to present yourself to customers in ways that build their empathy and their interest in being associated with you. Your company must be like a friend who cares about what they care about. And, on occasion, you must go to extremes to demonstrate it.

Extremes, particularly ones that do something extraordinary for someone in need, spread epidemically through social media, solidifying your base and gathering new converts in their wake. This all adds up to an entirely new duty in your Job at the Top. In today's social media–drenched climate, you need to seek out and act on opportunities to distinguish your business in extraordinary ways. You need to orchestrate remarkable moments that will be picked up by social channels, ones that your customers will care about. And these events may or may not have a lot to do with the actual functions, features, quality, price, service, and convenience of what you sell.

## Distinguish Your Company in Extraordinary Ways

At CARSTAR, we used our automobile body shops to restore an iconic muscle car, which we toured nationally as the centerpiece for golf events, car shows, and car washes on our franchisees' premises to raise funds for the Make-a-Wish Foundation. We paralleled our efforts with a strong social media campaign. The buzz and community following we built far exceeded the effects of our total marketing budget, distinguished us from every other body shop, and made employees proud to be part of our nationwide team.

# Chapter 21

## *Bad Goals*

Lots of people miss their goals. I've been one of them. Often. But we keep playing the game, bowing to the ritual. The "setters" of the goals attempt to place our targets just beyond what they think we'd accomplish on our own. The "accepters" of these goals walk away with a resigned shrug.

Goals are supposed to motivate us. In many instances, however, they achieve just the opposite. Even when the exercise allows us to set our own yardstick and then negotiate the outcomes, some of us don't feel compelled by these artificially constructed targets. There's something contrived about the whole process. Despite all the books that argue to the contrary, the fact is that many people just don't operate that way; some just aren't motivated by goals. And those who are don't understand that not everybody is like them.

Goal setting is a linear process, premised on the idea that a person can maintain focus over a goal horizon. When the horizons are long, the goal-setting approach also presupposes that the goal will still make sense at the end. Goals appeal to a left-brain, engineering mentality.

They're often anathema, however, to creative types, people whose walks through life aren't a series of straight lines. Instead, these right-brain thinkers wander and see patterns along the way.

Sometimes these patterns prove to be the keys to overwhelming successes that most others miss.

After reading a number of Walter Isaacson's biographies, I believe that Albert Einstein, Benjamin Franklin, and Steve Jobs were wired like these creative, meandering types. Goals for these people can be their biggest downfall. To them, goals are limits, imposed by someone else and designating artificially their highest and best ways to contribute to the organization's future. Goals for "creatives" are neither motivators nor opportunities for big pay-offs. Rather, they act as confirmation that their organizations fail to appreciate who they are and, intentionally or unintentionally, are setting them up for failure.

The key point is that both kinds of people—left-brain linear and right-brain wandering thinkers—are important in your business. Goals only work with one of these types, though. The methods for inspiring and motivating the others must be different, and they're not necessarily "spreadsheet-able" in the way that goal structures usually suggest.

Triangulating cues from Mike Toth, leader of one of the fashion world's top branding firms, and from others like him, it's clear that motivating creatives takes three kinds of actions from the person at the top.

The first is taking the time to help people see the big picture, to understand what's most important to the business over the long run and why. This is not about the financials, but rather about "the soul" of the business.

The second is modeling the behavior you seek. Most creative people are visual rather than auditory or numbers oriented. The best way to motivate them is to show them the processes and outcomes you're looking to create and help them imagine what it would feel like to do the same things themselves.

The third is to listen. Here you might consider initiating one of my old tricks: lunch with the CEO. Invite people to group lunches at which you update your big-picture thinking and ask for help in improving the images, as well as for ideas about moving forward. Encourage people to send you their thoughts, and make time to talk with them about their ideas. Take notes when they talk and review your notes in your sixty-minute sessions.

Sure, our investors, bankers, accountants, and half our staffs need goals. But one half of the organization is, at best, annoyed by the process.

Recognize the difference and use the right tools for the right job: you'll never sculpt a statue with a table saw.

# Chapter 22

## *Continuous Turnaround*

We've all heard about continuous turnarounds. These are the businesses everybody talks about, the ones constantly leaving everyone gasping in their tailwinds. Just about the time we figure out what they've done to set themselves so far ahead—they do it again. Da#* it! And still they baffle us. How do these companies do it? Could my company do it, too?

For me, the growing successes of continuous turnaround businesses signal a winding down of our legacy model for business performance. These old models are anchored in the ideas of stability, steady progress, and conservatism. However, today, one doesn't need to look hard to find examples of the new methods outpacing the old. One such example is Apple, which cannibalized its desktop computer with a laptop. Then it invented the iPod. Which it killed with the iPhone. Then it eclipsed all these devices with the iPad.

We see the same dynamic in small businesses that become big ones. Look, for example, at Jim McCann, who started as a social worker planting flowers as part of a therapy program. Then he went to work in a flower shop, which he eventually bought. To move to the next level, he turned his business into 1-800-Flowers, the first twenty-four-hour, seven-days-a-week, toll-free florist service. When the Internet rose as a business avenue, he moved his business online, with 1800flowers.com, becoming the single larg-est gift conglomerate in the United States.

Can a small or mid-size owner do the "Apple thing"? Well, sure! But how?

It starts at the top. If you're wondering why your business isn't like Jim McCann's, and whether it could be, go straight to the heart of the matter. Look in the mirror.

Mary Baker Eddy, a favorite thinker I mentioned earlier, said, *"We must form perfect models in thought and look at them con-tinually, or we shall never carve them out in grand and noble lives."*

My message to you is the same. Think, and you will become. Dream big. Make time in your life at work to be alone and con-template what you could be. Do this for sixty minutes three days a week. Then divest yourself of every activity that can be done by someone else. Follow your thinking. And *carve out grand and noble lives!*

# The Captain Has Turned Off
# the Seatbelt Sign

*Ladies and gentlemen, we have reached our cruising altitude at thirty-nine thousand feet, and the captain has just turned off the seatbelt sign. This is your signal that you are free to get up from your seats and move about the cabin.*

*We are expecting fair weather, a smooth ride, and an on-time arrival. So please use the remainder of our flight to shift your thoughts for the rest of your journey from how to think like a CEO to how to handle yourself like one.*

# Chapter 23

## *Accelerant for Your Thinking*

Up to this point, we have concentrated on the first half of the Job at the Top—*thinking* like a CEO. Doing a great Job at the Top has to start with your continuous, conscious attention to the whole of your business. Your sixty minutes three days a week builds your resolve about your company and about what it will take to move your business toward the future you intend.

Regardless of the acuity of your thinking, though, it will always be insufficient. You cannot drive your business to greatness on your own. You can't do it even with the full complement of your executive team. You need more people to support you, and they must give more than what it takes to keep their jobs. Ideally, everyone in your organization will be fully committed to you and to your cause.

Creating that reality depends more upon your own personal character than it does upon anything else.

Driving your business to true greatness depends upon zealous followers in every corner of your organization, from the highest-level executive to the newest and lowest-paid hourly worker. You need people who have internalized your ideas as their own, and who are committed to giving you everything they've got. Employees throughout your organization should be able to materialize your concepts into hard-hitting aspirations of their own. In fact, it's likely they'll contribute some exciting ideas along the way, things you'd never have thought of on your own, which can act as accelerants and multipliers of your intentions.

---

## Ways to Accelerate Thinking

Here are just a few examples of moves from the top that catapulted employee followership to new highs in companies I've run:

- At Bear Archery we built outdoor shooting venues so employees could test products at lunch and after hours, and we incorporated many of their insights into improvements that reflected the principles of the brand.
- At Dateq we turned over the reconfiguration of the IT platform to a panel of internal specialists and customer representatives.
- At Norcom we engaged the entire executive and supervisory team in the decision to trim the product line and focused the new plant configuration on developing an unassailable lead in the supply of notebook and paper-based school supply products to mass merchants.
- At MW Manufacturers, I, as CEO, rode delivery trucks, helped pack and unload windows, worked shifts as a line worker, and ate often in the plant lunchroom to bolster confidence in management and gather ideas from the front lines.
- At MW I polled our two thousand employees to find out what would make them most proud of our company. The answer was: a NASCAR sponsorship. We set a productivity goal, achieved it, and became lead sponsor

of a Busch Series car. Every toolbox on the plant floor and every vehicle in the parking lot carried the red #30 sticker!

- At CARSTAR I started an annual summit, a gathering of our franchisees, run by our franchisees, at which our entire executive team sat in the back of the hotel ballroom only to listen. They sat, not uttering a single word all day, absorbing sometimes hard-edged perspectives on what we could do to improve the lives of everyone our businesses touched.
- At Battery Solutions I began a Lunch with the CEO program for those at non-managerial levels to let me know what they liked most and least about the company and how we could make it better.

---

In short, what separates great companies from the also-rans is people who are devoted to helping you succeed. These impassioned employees work to their highest capacity because they trust and admire your character and they are committed to sharing in your successes.

The thinking half of your job is like preparing a car for a grand prix race. You need to know all there is to know about how the mechanical components fit together for optimum performance, about the handling characteristics of the car, and about the course to be driven.

The character part, then, is the driving. It's your style as you pilot the vehicle, and it's what inspires your pit crew and the crowd to stand and scream encouragement. Your personal character is the spark that has the power to ignite a fission-like, pervasive undercurrent of zeal.

But here's a word of caution: don't confuse character with appeal. Character has nothing to do with the way you look, how hard you work, or whether you're a great orator. It doesn't depend upon you being blessed with savoir faire or being the smartest person in the room.

Character is simply how much you care for others. It's how committed you are to those who have chosen to spend a large part of their lives as workers in your organization. It's about your commitment to your customers and your suppliers and everyone else your business touches. Character is how you show this commitment to all of these people.

Curiously, emphasizing this kind of character isn't a strong suit of our models for behavior in Jobs at the Top. It's not taught in schools, nor is it talked about much around the dinner table. Most of what anchors the approach to CEO jobs has to do with financial concepts: EBITDA, ROI, cash flow, and value creation. So little credence is given to elements other than the numbers that many of us have given up considering character as a relevant attribute of those at the top. The thinking is, "As long as the numbers are forthcoming, who cares?"

But one thing is certain. Inside most people remains a desire to believe in, and to admire, the person for whom they work. And when that admiration is justified, day in and day out, by the behavior of the CEO, the effects are amazing.

Facts support this argument. Read the literature about the most admired and most profitable companies in the world. The ideals they hold aren't rooted in the numbers; they're based on something else, something that inspires deeply committed followership. The response it generates is more visceral than the one that comes with moving a share price or making a few rich people richer. It's the feeling of supporting something that's wrapped in higher meaning and that is demonstrated, through both the easy times and the hard times, through consistent, admirable character at the top. That's what generates the numbers; it's not the other way around.

## *Fortune* Magazine's Top Ten Most Admired Companies in the World—2013

- Apple
- Google
- Amazon
- Coca-Cola
- Starbucks
- IBM
- Southwest Airlines
- Berkshire Hathaway
- Walt Disney
- FedEx

So, what are the attributes of that kind of character? And how do you demonstrate them? That's what the rest of chapters in this book are all about.

Like the chapters before these, you can take them in sequence or you can crack open the second half of the book and pick one at will. Either way, use these ideas as fuel for your sixty minutes alone three days a week. They'll add a dimension to the way you handle yourself that will extend and intensify your followership.

# Chapter 24

## *Authenticity*

Do you want your business to be extraordinary? I mean—*really* extraordinary?

It starts with you—but in a way that's different from what you've ever heard before, and a whole lot easier. Extraordinary accomplishment requires extraordinary commitment. Your own, yes, but also extraordinary commitment from others who believe in you and in your business. You must inspire employees to not just "trade" you their forty hours a week for pay, but to "gift" you with their zeal and help you succeed.

People only gift their zeal to one kind of person: one who's authentic. They will only follow a person in whom they believe. People particularly need a person who makes them feel part of something special and especially cared for.

It took me a while to figure this out, so I misspent some of my career trying to be admired rather than understood and believed. Sound familiar?

I felt like I was putting on a costume every day that didn't quite fit. But it was what I thought people needed to see. I even had some successes in that getup. Looking back, I see that those laurels were won by others, not by me. They were won by people in the organization who were better understood and in whom others believed. I was just the guy in the costume who happened to be standing in front of the parade at the right time.

So, are you authentic and believed in your organization?

Pause before you respond. A lot of people who shouldn't, answer "yes" right away. The phony at the top is always the last to know he's not admired by his colleagues. Why? Because when you're in the Job at the Top, your stature prevents most others from letting you in on how they actually see you. So, you go on with the show, believing that you're getting away with it while they roll their eyes and talk about you around the watercooler.

My own makeover—from a wannabe Bonaparte to an aspiring Braveheart—wasn't too difficult. But it did take a willingness to accept that I wasn't who I wanted to be at work. And it took a deep commitment to get it right.

Your journey starts with you deciding that you like yourself. It's the first step in allowing others to see you authentically. I got there by making a list of things I liked most about myself and comparing it to a list of things I hoped no one would ever find out about. It was a sobering moment.

My conclusion? The first list outweighed the second. That's good news, and your conclusion will probably be the same. But there definitely were items on the second list that embarrassed me, and that I needed to fix. After fixing the worst of my traits, I really didn't care whether people knew about the negatives that were left. There were enough positives in the first category to carry the day. After all, nobody's perfect.

Next, power up your "Phony Meter." It's the little device we all have that signals when we're trying to be someone other than who we really are. But we only hear it if we're listening. And many of us never turn it on.

When you first start paying attention, your Phony Meter goes off a lot. With time, as you begin to behave in accordance with your more authentic self, it will go off less frequently. At the same time, other people start to develop a better understanding of who you are—and you begin to feel deeper comfort and satisfaction.

There are no more tantrums when something goes wrong, even if it's your fault. You'll simply feel calm resolve to work through the problem, knowing that you're good, damn good. Your sense of who you are is solid, and there's nothing to hide.

The best part? Your belief in yourself is what's authentic to others. It's what they seek. They want to be inspired, to feel part of something special, cared about, and proud. Together, these feelings anchor a depth of followership that no guy in a costume can ever achieve.

So, what does it take to be your most authentic self? It takes a combination of courage and humility to learn how you are perceived, and to think hard about who you need to be in order to build the business you want. Once you know who you need to be, you must work to assiduously align your thinking and behavior with that persona. That's what creates an extraordinary company. It's all up to you!

Think about it. Sixty minutes three days a week.

# Chapter 25

## *Leadership Is an "Inside Job"*

Over the past decade, a single topic has dominated the business book shelves. It's leadership.

But has this focus on leadership done any good? My hunch: likely not as much as we'd hope, and it has maybe done some harm along with the good. Leadership isn't something you can "learn," like golf. It's not a new outfit you can put on or a set of new words and practices you adopt and use because they've been successful for others.

How-to prescriptions for leadership divert attention away from the seed at its core because leadership is not about how you act, what you say, or what you know. Nor is it about how those appearances play on the outside. Rather, it's about who you are on the inside.

As proof, great leaders come in all wrappings, with the most effective often appearing as the least probable successes. Most of them have never read the "Ten keys to leadership success" drivel that fills up our e-mails from business bloggers and self-appointed pundits' sites. For the best leaders, leadership is not learned, it's something they feel. It's not something they've added, because it was already there.

Take, for example, Joshua Lawrence Chamberlain, one of the most celebrated heroes of the Civil War. He defended Little Round

Top at Gettysburg with a hopelessly outnumbered force of Mainers, turning the tide of the battle and winning the Congressional Medal of Honor. A soft-spoken and studious college professor with no prior military experience, Chamberlain was perhaps the least likely hero of the war. After the war ended, he became the governor of Maine and followed his career in public service by becoming the president of Bowdoin College.

A more recent example is Russell Wilson, the Seattle Seahawks quarterback. Drafted as a backup, Russell drove himself to training camp in an old car along with all his belongings while other rookies flew. By the time he arrived, he'd memorized the entire playbook while his other rookie teammates thought they'd crack the manual at camp. He arrived early at every session and stayed late, and took humble interest in helping teammates who struggled with their new regimens and transitions into professional expectations. Through his character, Russell raised the spirit of the entire Seattle organization to new heights, both in the locker room and on the field. An extraordinarily gifted athlete, but also a reserved, committed, and authentic young man who refuses formal interviews unless he is dressed in a coat and tie, Wilson was the NFL coaches' choice for Rookie of the Year in 2012, and already has the following of a Hall of Fame player.

How did these leaders accomplish so much? They did it because of who they are. Anchored in a rock-solid internal sense of duty, they had an obsession to live up to their ideals; they put everything else second to their allegiance to what they believed was right.

You can get there too. It may require sacrifice. You may need to invest time and mind space. But if you care enough about being great at what you do—leading your organization from your Job at the Top—you won't be able to put that intention in second place. Think about it. Alone. Sixty minutes three days a week.

# Chapter 26

## *Humility Not Hubris*

O bserve a business owner's behavior long enough and you can paint a pretty accurate picture of what's driving her.

Business schools would say that the answer is profit. But profit is seldom what's really driving an owner. Sure, it's what we always talk about. But profit's a second-level motivator for most of us. It's a surrogate for something deeper...and often uncomfortable to talk about...that actually drives how we think and behave in our businesses. And it's that deeper motivator that determines our effectiveness as well as our ability to deliver profit.

The punch line here? What motivates many people who run businesses is *poison* to their intended success. The ones I see most are *fear* and its near opposite, *hubris*. Start looking, and you'll see them too. They are frequently demonstrated at the top, particularly in underperforming businesses.

Fear is a product of our instinct for preservation. It's impossible to shed it completely, nor do we want to. But many of us need to bring it into better balance.

Fear is most destructive where it's least visible. It's most damaging not when we're failing to stand up to an obvious challenge but rather when we hesitate to act on things that we believe, but aren't absolutely certain, could be right for our businesses. Or when we choose not to confront resistance to altering the way things have been done in the past. Or when we shy away from reasonable risk to avoid embarrassment or consequence if we're wrong.

The solution?

Adjust your thinking to see being wrong, within reasonable boundaries of risk, as a sign of your courage. You'll start thinking differently. Courage and the ability to see things others don't are why you get paid more than anyone else in your company. It's hard. It's risky. It's important. It's what makes the difference between great companies and all the rest. And it's no one's job but yours.

Follow through on that job and people will start seeing you in a brighter light, as an adventurer. As a person never satisfied with the status quo, always pushing for new things. Some of those things won't work, but they'll see you picking yourself up with a smile every time and heading off again. You're exciting to be around because you're not timid and you don't over-respond to fear.

Hubris, on the other hand, means extreme pride or arrogance. Like fear, it's a natural instinct, though it's found only among social animals. Unlike fear, hubris and domination of others often feels good to the perpetrator. Hubris in the extreme is a debilitating trait, and it is poison for organizational followership. Most unfortunate of all, the worst perpetrators seldom recognize it in themselves.

Fortunately, as with fear, there are pretty simple ways to bring hubris into check and use it as a positive force, one that turns people toward us rather than away.

To control hubris, you'll need a trusted partner, someone who is secure enough and has enough guts to give you the truth. And this is the raw, tough-minded, "make-you-angry" kind of truth. Find someone who can share that kind of truth and ask him to help you see yourself the way others see you.

Go slowly. Tackle only one attribute you'd like to change

at a time. Ask your discussion partner for specific examples of instances where you could have handled yourself more effectively. Request that he give you examples of times when your words or actions might have generated negative responses you likely missed. Ask for the names of people with whom you need to do a better job of building or repairing a trusting relationship. Seek advice in advance of key communications to the company for ideas about how to reposition yourself with regard to the attribute you are working on. Take a few minutes in your sixty minutes three times a week to reflect on your progress. Write down your assessment and check it with your partner. Continue the practice until a new consciousness starts to feel natural. Then ask your partner to help you tackle another attribute.

Fear and hubris are insidious problems. They're seldom evident to the perpetrators, partially because no one is going to tell the boss that she's insufferably arrogant or a coward. But these destructive traits also flourish because we have so few credible models that show us how to handle ourselves effectively in our Jobs at the Top.

Overcoming fear or hubris…and nearly all of us have some to conquer…really isn't too hard. And getting it done has big impacts for your business, if you've got the courage and humility to do something about it.

# Chapter 27

## *Moments of Truth*

"These are the times that try men's souls." I'm under no delusion that I'm Thomas Paine. And I know it's not 1776.

But from time to time we all face moments of truth in running our businesses. We all encounter situations that test our resolve for living according to the lofty principles we've talked about. When we handle them right, we inspire our troops to follow our lead and we offer motivation that lives on well beyond our moments of anguish, decision, action, and glory. Handling our challenges with authenticity and grace implants a force in our followers more powerful than anything else we could say or do. And it sets the incentive for others to do the same.

Our moments of truth aren't always big challenges, but they are situations where there's an easier way out, and where we have the opportunity to choose the higher, harder path. They're the moments when we put our jobs, and maybe even our whole companies, on the line for what we believe is right. They're also the moments when we earn our pay. Being at the pivot...calling the shots...on matters big and small telegraphs to everyone else what lies at the core of our company's value system.

Too few of us look hard enough for these opportunities. Partially, it's because there are always other things for us to do that make us feel like we're contributing. And partially it's because our natural instinct is to avoid, rather than seek, situations that test our resolve to match our actions with our high ideals. That's particularly true when that high ideal is a tougher path to walk.

A record of choosing higher right paths, however, is exactly what distinguishes your business from others in the eyes of your employees, your customers, your suppliers, and the communities you serve. It's what inspires admiration and, in turn, support from others when you need it most.

So, what does turning up our focus on moments of truth look like?

First you've got to recognize them. And for most of us, there are far more moments of truth arising every day in every corner of our organizations than we ever take note of. Careful reading between the lines of e-mails reveals some of these. I find them hidden between the lines in reports that well-intentioned colleagues send me of the decisions and actions they've taken. These are marvelous opportunities to ask—without any hint of reprimand—how what they've just related matches up with the high standards you've set for your company through its core values and purpose, and how it supports the mission and tangible images you're committed to achieving.

Just as you sharpen your acuity on things that interest you—like the moves of a professional athlete you admire, the makes and models of cars, architecture, or music—you can heighten your interest in seeking out instances to reinforce the "higher right" ethic in your business, and your attention to this will reveal ever more opportunities to do so. Once you commit to looking for them, you will find chances to reinforce your business's mission and values in one-on-one conversations, in formal and informal discussions with your team, and in conversations with outsiders when your team is present.

Your intention is to seek out moments of truth and act on them from your position in the Job at the Top, rather than taking the easier course of just letting them pass by. Your goal is to align the thought processes, decisions, and activities of your entire organization with your core values, your sense of purpose, your mission, and the tangible images you hold for the future of your business. But you can't be everywhere to enforce this. Nor can you impose yourself in ways that undermine effective delegation or others' responsibilities for their own jobs and for their own areas of your company, so your solution has to be more subtle. You can impress your values first by setting a clear example, then by teaching, and then by coaching. You can do it by going overboard to telegraph the alignment of your own words, actions, and decisions with what you believe is best for your company.

By demonstrating your own consistent focus on your core values and by continually seeking opportunities to reinforce your own commitment through your own moments of truth, you'll be teaching everyone else to do the same.

Does your company lack a spelled-out set of core values, purpose, mission, and tangible images? They are not too hard to put in place. They're already "in the woodwork" of most organizations, just neglected. Your job is to resurrect them and make them apparent in your own, and thereby in other people's, lives.

Gather a team for forty-five minutes and ask them to finish these sentences:

"At (our company) we believe deeply in…"
"We make the world a better place by…"
"Over the next _____ months we shall become…"
"Then in our business lives we will enjoy…"

If you need examples of solid core values, purpose, mission, and tangible images, go back to the sidebar in chapter 17, "Your Goggles for Greatness," for those that make up the vision at Battery Solutions.

It'll take a few sessions, but soon you'll be zeroing in on a crisp statement of vision, one that stir emotions both for the values that everyone wants to protect and for the next heroic milestone everyone wants to achieve. Then, the aligned moments of truth will blossom throughout your organization.

# Chapter 28

## *Thermonuclear Influence*

It's easy to get carried away with ourselves in our heady Jobs at the Top.

We're all susceptible to hubris, to some degree. But your degree of susceptibility depends upon your level of comfort with yourself. Getting carried away with ourselves is a greater risk if we are hiding something about who we are, and pretending to be something we're not. If we feel we need trappings to indicate our worth, we may not be comfortable with who we are.

It took me a long time to understand this point. The people who are generally the most difficult to be around—loud, bossy, arrogant, unsympathetic, aloof, self-absorbed, ungracious—usually like themselves least. Their behaviors, which are so destructive in organizational contexts, are really mechanisms they deploy to keep people from seeing their flaws.

Why is this significant? Because organizational effectiveness exists in inverse proportion to pretensions at the top. And it's parallel to openness and selflessness.

The prescription for turning up the pace of an organization from complacent to thermonuclear isn't what most people think. In fact, it's just the opposite. Panic, fear, and exhortation might get a short response, but never one that lasts. What does? Humility. Particularly when humility at the top is coupled with openness and courage. A leader should be open to having her ideas challenged and improved upon. She must be grateful to be proven wrong, and have the courage to stand her ground, at all personal costs, for what she believes is right for her business. Everyone loves an effective leader who is humble, and they'll do everything they can to make their humble CEO succeed, possibly because these types of leaders are so few and far between.

Humble CEOs never take themselves too seriously. They are serious about the business, yes, but not about themselves. They're brutally committed to the needs of their businesses without letting their dedication spill over to self-importance. And they never make others feel inferior, avoiding distinctions and perks that set them above the rest.

So, how do you become such a CEO? It's a matter of will.

It takes a willingness to see yourself at the point of the pyramid, but with the point facing down, not up! (Read more about this in the next chapter.) You need to see your role as setting up circumstances that allow your employees to function at their best. You need to create conditions that prime your people to give your business all they've got, so that they are more effective in your organization than they could be anywhere else. You want them to feel proud to be associated with your company—and proud of themselves and their roles in achieving the outcome you are committed to.

Some of the ways I create an atmosphere of common commitment include:

- Taking a small office with nothing in it that doesn't relate directly to my job—no trophies, no golf or fishing pictures.
- Touring the plant every day, and sometimes eating in the plant lunchroom.
- Wearing the company shirt, answering my own phone, and making my own coffee and copies.

- Arriving early, staying late, parking in the back of the lot, and not driving a fancy car to work.
- Looking people in the eye and remembering their names and something important about them... and taking notes when they talk.
- Listening more than talking in meetings, asking questions, summarizing others' ideas, and doing what I say I'll do.
- Signing Christmas and birthday cards and including a note telling people how glad I am to work with them. A thousand a year is not too many... I've done it and it's worth it!

Think about how well you measure up to this standard in your sixty minutes alone three days a week.

# Chapter 29

## *Flip the Pyramid*

I hate them. They're egotistical. And they cap, rather than inspire, motivation. The rant this time? It's organizational charts! You know the ones I'm talking about—they start with the owner at the top and everyone else fanning out below. These boxes show company titles inside that string along, from the highest box to more and more boxes, multiplying both down and across a landscape page.

The most effective owners these days—the ones beating the pants off everyone else—see it just the other way, with themselves occupying the point of the triangle, but at the bottom. These revolutionists embrace a higher understanding of how organizations work best, and they truly understand how to get the best out of the individuals who work for them. The number of traditional top-down businesses delivering exceptional results is declining.

Along with the traditional pyramid, the term "reporting to" is past its useful life. But many of us still see the chain of command as a law of nature, as the imperative and unarguable connective tissue for organizational design. It isn't anymore.

This idea of command rose from military discipline. There, the individual troop isn't expected to be smart enough to figure out on his own how to contribute to a win on the battlefield. Nor is he expected to be reliable enough to put himself at mortal risk for the cause when it's necessary that he do so. Hence, came the "reporting to" structure and accompanying grave consequences for disobedience. Henry Ford reflected this idea when he asked, "Why is it every time I ask for a pair of hands they come with a brain attached?"

Ford had a lot of great ideas, but that wasn't one of them. Still, his comment was understandable given the thinking about work at that time. On the assembly line, people were largely substitutes for machines. Variation from stridently established procedures meant inefficiency. What's not so understandable is why the idea persists in so many of our businesses today, though thinking and creativity have become the greater substance of nearly everyone's work.

Maybe it's because it feels good to be at the top of the food chain and have others "report to" us. Or maybe it's because some of us still think we're smarter than anyone else. Or maybe, simply, because that's the model we've inherited, the one everyone else uses, and the only one we've ever seen demonstrated.

To be truthful, I think we are all susceptible to these influences. Take just a moment and think about yourself: How susceptible are you? If you admit you are, what can you do about it? And what might you expect as a result?

Here's what I do, and what I've experienced. Every time. I start by drawing my org chart upside down, with me at the bottom and with the sales team across the top. I do this because I see my job as helping everyone else to make her highest contribution. The proof of my success comes in high-profit sales. Furthermore, if I truly understand my job, and I understand sales, I've got the best chance of seeing the relevance of everything else that lies in between *from the point of the pyramid on up!*

Then I spend most of my time thinking about how to catalyze others to achieve higher productivity on their own. I do this by experimenting and setting up circumstances that encourage them to find their highest potential, which also throws out our legacy structures for job descriptions.

Situations that motivate smart people don't put them in boxes or categorize them on spreadsheets. Nor do they limit individuals to "reporting to" someone else.

Smart people want a runway that's at least partially open, with latitude and resources to develop themselves on their own. This places a greater burden on me, as CEO, to make sure that everyone understands the fundamentals of my whole business, the roles of the parts, points of advantage for our market, and our competitive positioning.

At the same time, I need to trade in my bullhorn for a giant catcher's mitt and trade my instinct for enforcement for a passion to receive well-intended inputs. And I must incorporate these inputs into my own relentless search for new patterns toward a better business without losing track of my duty to keep my business performing optimally.

What should you expect? It'll take a while for you to shift into this mode of pushing from the bottom. Start with a small project that has a short time frame and limited risk. Set the expectations, provide the resources, and let your team figure out how to make it happen. Provide help when asked. When that's successful, go a little bigger—until the news of how you're operating touches your entire company.

Then you'll see a spike of enthusiasm. A culture will emerge that seeks, rather than avoids, change. This culture will support people who work together in a way that puts a new multiplier on the idea that the whole is greater than the sum of its parts.

# Chapter 30

## *The Last to Know*

It's lonely at the top." We've heard that characterization so many times that we don't even bother to question its wisdom. Furthermore, we accept it, because for far too many of us it's true. But for a fortunate few, it isn't.

CEOs in this latter category feel something different. They embrace warmth and protection from a position as centerpiece of a community of alignment, optimism, and well-being. It's the exact opposite of the anxiety lived by those of us who stand in the buffer zone between our organizations and the parties with financial interests in the business, who are never quite satisfied with the outcomes we achieve.

I've been in both spots, and upon reflection, the experiences I've felt at either extreme have had a lot more to do with my own sense of self in guiding a business than with its performance. Will you be a lonesome overlord laboring to satisfy those with financial interests in the business? Or will you be a community builder, confident that a solid job in that area will yield all other satisfactory results? My take? It's a matter of choice.

What is it that puts CEOs onto the track of isolation as overlords? What's the alternative path to becoming a centerpiece? And can an "overlord" make the transition?

First, what drives so many to isolation? The key that opens the door to deep satisfaction in the Job at the Top isn't what most people think it is. It's not what we're taught in school about how to succeed, about how to lead, or about how to ensure a life of abundance. The messages from all of those portals center on being smarter than anyone else, knowing things that others don't, and using that knowledge to elevate ourselves above the pack and, thereby, get things done that others can't.

The result is egocentricity and hubris, which wall us off from our organizations. This is a situation that the constituencies on both sides may wish were different, but which they just accept as the way things are.

Part of the resulting tragedy is personal for the CEO, but the other part affects everyone else the business touches. The personal tragedy is that walled-off CEOs, when they wander off track, as we all do from time to time, are the last ones to know! In the past two and a half decades of advising underperforming businesses, I've never found one where people in the ranks didn't sense trouble for their CEO and talk about it among themselves before the occupant in the Job at the Top acknowledged it. Sadly, in many cases, by the time the CEO became aware, it was too late to do anything about it.

Why? Because the CEO was sending "I'm smarter than you" signals to everyone, indicating that constructive criticism wasn't welcome and that the mantle of "greater smarts" would carry the business through.

It's tempting to write off this phenomenon as intellectual arrogance, simply a natural trait common to people who make it to the top. But I don't buy that assessment because I've seen individuals of every emotional persuasion fall victim to the trap. The cause is the widely held and misguided belief that in order to guide the organization, the person in the Job at the Top must sit on a plane of wisdom that's higher than everyone else's. When we defer to this seat of wisdom, we miss the opportunity to tap the collective wisdom of our organizations. In many instances, drawing from the insights of the group could help the company avoid trouble that ends up being endured by all.

Now, what's the alternative path? How, as CEO, do you avoid isolation? How do you be a centerpiece CEO rather than an exile? It's not too difficult, but does require that you change how you see yourself in your Job at the Top.

Rather than casting yourself as the high oracle, a modern-day Solomon, CEOs who tap the full wisdom of their organizations see themselves as the "head learner," the one with the insatiable desire to know more and who is willing to learn from everyone else. These CEOs thrust aside the false and thin mantles of wisdom and position themselves as the individuals constantly reaching out to others, regardless of organizational position, for help in understanding the whole of their business.

"Centerpiece" CEOs are constantly interacting with others in ways that "isolationists" avoid at all costs. Centerpiece CEOs say:

- "I really hadn't thought that, but would love to hear more."
- "I've been thinking about something for a while and am stuck. Would you help me?"
- "It seems to me that there's something going on here that's holding us back. What do you think?"

If you are an "I can't be wrong," isolationist kind of person, you'll be missing at least half of the joy of running your business. It's the joy that comes from knowing that you are deploying the intellectual power of the business to its fullest extent in moving your cause forward. It's the relief of shedding the idea that the responsibility is all yours. It's shedding the fear of being wrong—we're all wrong every now and then, and that's okay. And it's the joy of seeing pride and initiative in the faces of those around you rather than dull resignation to ideas and actions that they know won't work out.

So, you can be an intellectual isolationist or the centerpiece in a community of wisdom. It's a choice. Yours.

# Chapter 31

## *Volunteers Versus Employees*

I often hear senior CEOs asking, "What's the deal with the people who work in my company these days? The generations X, Y, next, and millennials? They just aren't committed to their jobs like we were. And they expect things to come along with work—free—that never crossed our minds. It can't all be due to video games and bad parenting."

The actual diagnosis is pretty simple. It's both of us—the older generations and the younger generations—together. We sometimes appear like oil and water. Helium and a spark.

### Older Versus Younger Thinking

| Older | Younger |
|---|---|
| Security | Challenge |
| Advancement | Recognition now |
| Living by the rules | Freedom to improvise |
| Having a good life | Making meaningful differences |

From the senior CEO side, some of us continue to see the people who work in our organizations as we have in the past—as *employees*. We think they ought to be grateful to us for giving them a paycheck and that they ought to express their gratitude by doing what's needed and what they're told. And they should do it with loyalty and enthusiasm.

But many younger workers see themselves quite differently— as *volunteers*. They seek work where they feel they are appreciated, where they can make a difference they feel good about, and where their own choices and consent are valued. They don't view their employment as simply a transaction that gives them pay for compliance. Rather, they view themselves as valuable resources who can make important contributions, but who aren't always appreciated. Even in this economy, they expect positions where their talents will be well received and magnified, and where their passions, their ingenuity, and their ideas about furthering a cause they respect will be lauded.

The message for us all? Time doesn't go backward!

The days of command and control, and compliance in exchange for pay, are over. If we are to motivate our younger workers, we need to see them and their work through their lens. We must begin to see them not as fungible placeholders in rigid structures but rather as individuals with unique desires and, in many cases, far higher potential to contribute than we ever might have imagined. And we must remember that they have choices, as volunteers, not employees.

Even pay, the "fail-safe" sledgehammer in our tool kit for compliance, isn't what it used to be. Up-and-coming generations expect fair compensation. But pay—even a high salary with lucrative incentives for exceptional performance—has lost a lot of its punch. Recent surveys of high-potential seniors in high schools and colleges reinforce this fact, documenting a surprising willingness among this group to accept 15 percent to 30 percent less in salary in order to work in a place they admire. Even in this challenging economy!

Widespread willingness to value meaningful work over pay sounds disorienting at first to most of us over the age of forty-five, but it's really not surprising. Adjusting your business to these new realities, and to the substantial benefits of smarter people working harder and more creatively for you, starts with you. It starts with your willingness to let go of the way you've thought about personnel in the past, so you can create a company that people in their twenties, thirties, and early forties see as a superior fit with the things they care most about in their lives.

Your business must be a place where those individuals who choose to spend their time with you feel inspired and proud to serve, a place where they want to give you their all.

How do you create such an environment? By setting a standard for yourself that warrants your people's admiration and commitment, and by being the model that settles for nothing less. Steve Jobs was famous for this. He set outrageous standards for product design, and he accepted nothing less than extraordinary results.

You don't have to run a business like Apple to apply the same methods. Nor do you need to be as notoriously irascible as Jobs was. In fact, you can be entirely considerate and kind, but nonetheless extreme in following his example in the drive for perfection, whether you're creating life-changing technology or repairing shoes.

The point is that admiration for your business follows your own admiration for your business, and for your volunteers. It's backed up by your own relentless demonstration of the standard you expect to be met by everyone else.

That kind of admiration only flows downhill, and it must start with you. Its descending wake gathers up passionate followership among today's volunteers, who will seek to give you more than you ever expected from an employee.

It's worth thinking about in your sixty minutes three days a week.

# Chapter 32

## *Duty Versus Responsibility*

When I talk to CEOs about the gravity of their jobs, many bemoan their burdens and responsibilities. They talk about what they "owe"—to boards, investors, lenders, customers, and employees. But that's a trap, one set by those just mentioned. It ensures that their interests are highest on your obligation list, and even higher on your guilt list when things go wrong. And most of us step right into the trap.

The result is that we direct our attention to the wrong things. We divert our energy toward the concerns of others rather than toward what we know is most important for our business. We focus on spreadsheets rather than customers, for example. We spend far too many days preparing for far too regular board meetings rather than on customer calls or on simply thinking, quietly, about our businesses.

How do we break the cycle? It's easy. Start considering your obligation to your business as a duty rather than a responsibility. Duty is different from responsibility, particularly in its effect on your approach to your job. Responsibility comes from the outside. It's transactional. "I've done something for you, and now you have an obligation to me." It's also usually quantifiable, not too different from an indenture, which, on the bright side, you can shed once you've met its terms. But as long as you are susceptible to the grip of responsibility, you won't get rid of it. As soon as you check one responsibility off your list, it's likely to be replaced by another. Or maybe more.

Shift gears and imagine instead a standard of duty. Duty comes from the inside. It's not transactional, it's moral. And it derives from a clear understanding of the principles by which you intend to live your life. It's neither quantifiable nor time-bound. And yours is the only opinion that matters when it comes to measuring yourself against a standard of duty.

A clear sense of duty supersedes any burden of responsibility imposed upon you by someone else. Your sense of duty says, in effect, "If I live up to my higher calling, everything else will be taken care of, appropriate to its alignment with what's best for my business."

Living up to the call of duty protects you from diverting interest away from what you know really makes a difference. And a clear sense of duty gives you the backbone to stand up to anyone who challenges what you know is best for the future of your company.

Duty, not responsibility, is your greatest source of power at the top. Take a few moments in each of your sixty-minute sessions to work on a statement of duty.

Take your time. There's no rush. This can be the work of hours, weeks, or, in some cases, months. Allow simmering time. Allow time for each word to materialize and settle. Allow your collection of words to resonate deeply inside you until the moment that a proclamation arises and literally lifts you off your seat. You'll know you have it when, head cocked back, walking around the room, you repeat your statement of duty as if preaching to a riveted audience, like you're delivering the Gettysburg Address.

*"My solemn duty is to_____."*

Don't stop until you get there. Because once you get it right, it never leaves you. Once you've got a statement of duty that resonates, it will serve you continually as a moral compass that lets you discern responsibilities you'll accept, because they align with your unswerving sense of duty.

The catch? The only way to get there is alone. Thinking deeply. And a great time for that? Sixty minutes three days a week!

# Chapter 33

## *Go for Broke*

Particularly in this shaky economy, far too many of us have become "min-maxers," approaching our Jobs at the Top in a way that minimizes the maximum risk. We've learned to justify a "tail-between-the-legs" versus an "on-the-balls-of-our-feet, center-of-the-ring" stance.

But nearly everyone's competitive environment includes a rival who is thinking differently. Your rival may be taking ground that is not damaging you at the moment, but which you wish you were taking instead. I'll bet, without even thinking, you can name the company in your industry that is grabbing ground. To that company, your "min-maxing" is the ultimate easy layup. It's a free steak dinner. You are one of the rabbits in the presence of the tiger, and you hope he'll continue to overlook you.

Often, we write off the tigers as irrational. They just don't understand our business and how difficult it is these days. And they will eventually run out of steam. But trade places with a tiger for just an instant. Look at yourself through its yellow eyes. Is there any more attractive time for seizing advantage than when one's rivals are holding back, on their heels, and playing not to lose?

## Tigers Versus Rabbits

| Tigers | Rabbits |
|---|---|
| Sony | Zenith |
| Apple and Samsung | Motorola |
| Amazon | Department stores |
| McDonald's | Jack in the Box |
| JetBlue | US Airways |
| Netflix | Movie theaters |

My advice? Stop feeling subject to your circumstances! They are what they are. Go back to the days when you started. And...

*Go for broke! Again!*

Screw up your courage in your sixty-minute sessions three days a week. Determine the boldest moves you can survive, assuming all of them go wrong. Assign priorities. Let people know what's going on. And give 'em a rip!

When one strategy doesn't work, learn what you can from the experience, rest up, collect your strength, and launch another. This kind of boldness is the opposite of the methodical planning you might do in more prosperous, predictable, and easier times. But it's the perfect approach for these more precarious days. I call this process "assertive trial and error." Go small, but go frequent. Because when one of your ideas does hit, the impact is likely to be big, with the kind of success that elevates you to the ranks of the tigers. It's a big negative for the rest of the rabbits.

Think in your sixty-minute sessions about going for broke. Not only will you find ways to enhance, and maybe even to entirely transform your business, you'll spur soaring enthusiasm in the ranks. *If* you prepare your organization for a period of experimentation, that is. Assure them that you can afford a bumpy road to a better business. Warn them that you'll be asking them to try new things. Let them know that not all the ideas will work. And let them know you've decided that fighting back will feel a whole lot better than sitting there waiting for the tiger!

# Chapter 34

## *Your Uber Weapon—Emulation!*

Here's a concept that comes, curiously, as a surprise to many people in Jobs at the Top:

*You are the strongest force in your business!*

Think about it, candidly and honestly, in your sixty minutes alone three days a week. Are you fully exerting your force? If you can't answer with conviction, *YES*, then you're not doing your job well enough. It's as simple as that.

Take heart. Most people aren't. But most can. Those who believe unquestionably in themselves and in the nobility of what they're trying to accomplish in and for their organizations can become the strong forces their businesses need.

Don't mistake this discussion for an argument about style. Any number of different styles—as long as they are anchored in love of self and love of duty—will work, from that of the "scorch the earth" gladiator to that of the soft-spoken pacifist. It's not your angle of attack that counts. It's your own deep confidence in who you are, as well as your unassailable belief in the goodness of your mission. Those two attributes drive the degree to which the rest of your organization reflects and is inspired by who you are, top to bottom.

Said differently, we'd all be better off if our business book-shelves were full of titles on "followership," not leadership. The Job at the Top is to demonstrate clear motivation and ideals for followers, and to weed out those who don't fit. Cohesive organizations, regardless of style at the top, have power. Divided ones don't.

How do you make your organization cohesive? By capitalizing on a common trait of human nature.

*The power of emulation!*

People who work for you want two things: clear signals of character at the top of the organization and confidence that they are part of something inspired and important. Regardless of your style, if you're unwavering on both these fronts, the power of emulation kicks in! Not only will others be encouraged to be like you, but outliers will also be purged. Some will leave of their own choosing. And when you help the reluctant to either get on board or move out, your actions will peg the applause-o-meter.

If that's not what's going on in your organization, it's because you're wavering on one or both fronts.

In either instance, the power of emulation, and the degree to which it's working for you, is worth your conscious monitoring and attention during your sixty minutes three days a week. If the number of employees who are emulating you is high, think about why that is and how you can keep those numbers up. If it's not, think about where the flaw lies. Is it your confidence in yourself? Or are you wavering in your soulful commitment to your organization's intention?

Also think about how much you love yourself and about how much you love what you are trying to get done.

Are you worthy of emulation? Continue asking yourself that question, because nearly everyone can reach the point at which, if they think about it enough, they can stand up and shout, *YES!*

# Chapter 35

## *Be the Lore*

We love stories about others who inspire us, because stories about those kinds of people allow us to imagine that we're just like them. It's why we watch sports. It's why we buy *People* magazine. It's why we have heroes.

Your employees are no different. They seek to be inspired, even at work. They thirst for the thrill of being part of an organization led by someone they want to be more like, someone who has the courage, wisdom, tenacity, and tenderness they wish they had. They want to be able to tell tales of admiration to their families and friends, and they want their association with you and your company to make them feel special.

The sad truth is that few people are fortunate enough to work in organizations where such a force exists. Maybe that's why so few businesses are truly extraordinary: the seat of the head "story-maker" is empty. That void is one of the main reasons I contend that the Job at the Top is seldom done well enough.

So, your Job at the Top includes giving your people stories... about you. Stories of cleverness, heroism, selfless commitment, and caring that they'll be proud to retell to their families and friends. Provide them with stories that allow them to imagine they're just like you, and give them stories that inspire them to actually be like you. By consciously seeking opportunities to demonstrate, in the extreme, what your business stands for and how you'd like your people to be, you can deliver the lore they need and be the leader they swell with admiration to serve.

But be careful. Stories cut both ways. They can raise you on a pedestal to a stature that you then have to maintain. Or, if chosen poorly, stories can flatten you, leaving you bloody nosed and alone in the back corner of the parking lot at dusk.

The stories you want to tell are the ones that emphasize alignment with the business principles you want reflected by your people. Your stories shouldn't waver from that guideline, of reinforcing the choices and behaviors you want those in your organization to embrace. Avoid the stories that exalt only yourself and have little to do with your organization. The right stories are about you serving your business, not promoting yourself.

Take time to clarify the lesson you want learned. Find space in your sixty minutes three days a week to think about the legends who inspired others best. It's no mystery why General George Patton, leading the U.S. Second Armored Division in WWII, stood in the turret of the lead tank on assault, chrome battle helmet gleaming in the sun, riding crop held high at salute. General Patton did not have a death wish. Rather he knew that his valor at supreme moments of truth would inspire his army to greatness. Patton's division defeated the dreaded German *Afrika Korps* in Tunisia, a feat his army likely would never have achieved without his conscious attention to creating lore, behind which his troops rallied.

Similarly, it's no mystery why Herb Kelleher, founder and former CEO of Southwest Airlines, became the ultimate "fun guy." Pitted against a difficult financial, regulatory, and competitive environment, Kelleher launched his airline under the principles of service and the competitive advantage of the customer experience he intended to offer. He was an astute student of the airline industry, and he knew people hated air travel's poor on-time performance, uncomfortable seats, and most of all, indifferent treatment by airline employees. Kelleher's fledgling Southwest set new standards for timeliness and passenger comfort at coach rates.

But, most importantly, he established a culture of optimism and fun with his own antics, like hiding in overhead luggage compartments and dressing up as a female flight attendant. It's no accident that Southwest is often the most profitable operation in the air. Both George Patton and Herb Kelleher acted consciously to inspire others to replicate their own devotion to the principles of their organizations.

Start identifying opportunities where you can demonstrate extreme alignment with the way you want your business to be. Don't fear going overboard if you're jumping off the right side of your ship. Your intention should be to inspire your employees, customers, suppliers, business partners, banker, investors—and, yes, even your competitors' employees!

Be the lore. Give people what they need. Plus...it's a lot of fun!

# Touchdown

*Ladies and gentlemen, we have just touched down for an early arrival at Exemplary Field in the great City of Exceptional. I want to thank each and every one of you for choosing Transformation Airlines for your flight today. On behalf of our entire Exceptional-based crew, it has been a pleasure to serve you today in our transit from Averageville. Now that we are here, I can tell you that a dangerous weather system was headed for Averageville and I am glad we were able to get you out safely and on time.*

*Please stay seated with your seatbelts fastened for the short remainder of our trip.*

*When we reach the jetway I will turn on the cabin lights, signaling that it is safe to stand, gather your belongings, and exit the aircraft.*

*Once again, it has been a pleasure to serve you, and we wish you health and success, wherever your future travels may take you.*

# Chapter 36

## *The "L" Word*

L ove is a word we seldom use in business. But if you peel back the wrapping from emulation—your highest-voltage tool for building followership—you'll find love. Love for you, the leader, makes your organization want desperately to support your initiatives. Fear ensures only their compliance. Love releases their selfless zeal.

How do you get your people to love you? First, you must love yourself enough to be open, humble, approachable, wrong at times, and still confident. Then, you have to love what you want to achieve.

So, what's the difference between admirable love for yourself and conceit? Between love for what you're trying to make happen and selfishness? It's motivation. But it's an angle of motivation we mostly suppress, because it so directly challenges everything we've always heard about the purpose of our Job at the Top and about why our business exists.

Hang me from the yardarm, if you will. But I think we all know, deep inside, that profit's not a fundamental motivator. Making rich guys richer, even if it includes ourselves, isn't what inspires love. But love for us and our businesses is what fuels extraordinary accomplishment.

The root of organizational love is making a contribution that's needed, one that others aren't fulfilling or that we can do better. Whether it's altruism, pride, or a combination of both, doing something better is the soul of motivation to excel. And doing it for a cause that benefits someone else, as well as ourselves, is the magnum-force multiplier.

Imagine what it would feel like if everyone in your organization came to work filled with the desire to improve someone else's life. And improved their own at the same time!

You can make this happen. The nature of your business doesn't matter. It's all about how you see your business from your Job at the Top. It's in how you speak about it, what you reward, and how you justify your actions. It's in what you care about most, and whether that's making life safer, more affordable, or more enjoyable for others.

Try thinking about your business this way. Start talking about it. I bet you'll see signs of a springtime, with new energy around something that starts with "L."

# Chapter 37

## *Trust*

It's only fitting that this last chapter cover a topic that eclipses all the others under its umbrella: the eighteen chapters on how to think like a CEO and the thirteen on how to handle yourself like one. This topic is *trust*.

Trust is the capstone for everything that's come before. The messages of the first half of this book add up to a prescription for how to be trusted as the one who thinks at the highest level on behalf of the organization. *Trust* works just as well as a headline for the second half. The messages in the second part of the book offer a prescription for how to manage your behavior so you can catalyze the kind of commitment on the part of others that is requisite for extraordinary accomplishment.

Trust, therefore, is a perfect omnibus objective.

So much so that if someone asked me for a single exercise to shift my mind-set from the confusion of most days into the right frame of mind for sixty minutes alone, I would answer: "Ask simply, 'How well am I trusted?'" But this is only a preamble to a more important question: "How much *should* I be trusted?"

This second question is the kicker. It's a question that takes real courage, coupled with love of self, to confront openly and honestly. Because it's far too easy to trick oneself and others with the first question—and I suspect that we all can think of far too many CEOs who spend their lives attempting to do just that.

Getting to the point of acknowledging the second question is a challenging path for many people. This includes many, if not most, sitting CEOs. Asking yourself that question—in harsh and full light—is hard. But it may be even harder to accept the universal right answer:

> *How much should I be trusted? Less than*
> *I am ... perhaps far less.*

The raw truth is that once you're put in charge of a company or a part of one, you are in a job for which you will never be good enough. Your safest and most admirable posture, then, is to accept that truth and focus your emotions and your energy on narrowing the gap. Be kind and grateful whenever you are commended for your work, but never let that kind of feedback mutate into a misconception that you are finished with getting better.

One reason we're never done is that the job is complex. Even the simple Back of the Envelope exercise from chapter 7 is something you'll never finish. There's always more to know, and each dimension is always changing.

The other reason you're never finished with getting better is that what you do is supremely important. Not just to your banker, your investors, and your own well-being, but to the lives and families of everyone your business touches. And you will never be good enough to warrant the trust they have placed in you.

So, as you prepare for each of your sixty-minute sessions alone three times a week, take a moment to think about your duty of trust. It will inspire you like nothing else to be better. And better. And better.

You'll seek to warrant the trust of the noble souls who have decided to support you. And those relentless desires will sustain you, both spiritually and professionally. Through your quest, you will find yourself doing better in your Job at the Top. Along the way you just might even find yourself more satisfied in your personal life. One thing is for sure; it's something to think about in your sixty-minute sessions.

Good luck. I've done it. And I know that you can, too!

# Index

# About the Author

**Dick Cross** has worked with underperforming companies for more than 25 years, helping mainstream businesses get "unstuck" to achieve their next level of success. Dick has been the Chairman, CEO, or President at nine of those companies, and has mentored more than 100 CEOs at others. Much of his career has been spent in private equity circles, including Fenway Partners, and he currently serves on the board of numerous corporate, philanthropic, and civic organizations.

Early in his career, Dick worked with the management consulting firm The Cambridge Research Institute (CRI), and later joined the Berwick Group, a start-up, Boston-based general management consulting firm focusing on strategic planning. The focus of his work there was diagnosing and addressing companies' shortfalls in strategic and financial business performance. The beginnings of his *Just Run It!* framework began to take shape.

At Fenway Partners, Dick continued to perfect his craft. The prospectus for Fenway was to acquire and fix under-performing businesses. Since that time, Dick has gone on to run eight companies and to help dozens more turn around. Most recently, as Chairman and CEO of CARSTAR, a business that he steered from insolvency to a hugely successful recapitalization valued at ten times earning, Dick once again proved the success of his Just Run It! approach. During that time he also served as a Chairman or Director of a number of other business and philanthropic organizations.

Dick is an enthusiastic, colorful, and engaging speaker, who greatly enjoys conveying the story behind every business. He holds an undergraguate degree from the University of Virginia School of Architecture, a graduate degree from the Harvard Graduate School of Design, and a Masters of Science in business from Columbia University. He and his wife split the year between Concord, Massachusetts, and Gloucester Point, Virginia.